"The authors and translator have produced a richly a⟨...⟩ day language... This texture of being true to life will make it among ⟨...⟩ go-to books in the field of the dynamics of working organizations. It plumbs the depth of the love and loneliness that we all enjoy and suffer at work and provides a key chapter on the usefulness of psychoanalytic theory to tell us where to look."

- **Richard Morgan-Jones, psychoanalytic psychotherapist and consultant; author of** *The Body of the Organisation and its Health*

"The themes of love and loneliness as fundamental dimensions of life in organizations have been curiously under-examined until now. This book provides the remedy... There is something compelling about the way the authors have used love and loneliness to take the reader on a deep (yet very accessible) dive into the emotional life of organizations and why it matters. This book is bound to become a classic!"

- **Brigid Nossal, Deputy CEO & Director Consulting NIODA**

Love and Loneliness at Work

Love and loneliness, in both their presence and absence, are key aspects of our lives – including our working lives.

Love and Loneliness at Work offers an accessible and practical starting point for understanding the connections between emotions, individual working life and organizations, focusing on love and loneliness. The book begins with an engaging chapter-length case study that illuminates the themes discussed. Taking a psychodynamic perspective, Bonnerup and Hasselager examine love and how it influences our feelings about tasks, organizations and participation, as well as uniquely exploring pairs in working life. The book explores loneliness as an inner state of mind, as an aspect of the professional role and as a group dynamic experience, and assesses the psychological burden of feeling lonely in an organization. Bonnerup and Hasselager also provide an overview of key theoretical concepts, including the unconscious, anxiety, libido, projective processes and the concepts of inner and outer self, providing the tools required to examine, understand and work with the emotional strength and vulnerability of an organization.

This book provides unique insights into how understanding these feelings can help leaders, decision makers and employees contribute to healthier and happier workplaces. It will be an essential guide for coaches in practice and in training, as well as leaders and managers, human resources (HR) and Learning & Development (L&D) professionals and consultants within organizations seeking to expand their understanding of organizational dynamics. With its strong theoretical base, it will also be of interest to academics and students of coaching, coaching psychology, psychodynamic consulting, organizational psychology, leadership and management and organizational change, and to anyone seeking an insight into the emotional dynamics of working life.

Birgitte Bonnerup and **Annemette Hasselager** are psychologists and qualified supervisors in organizational psychology. They are partners in Bonnerup & Hasselager, where they work as organizational psychologists and therapists with individuals, groups and organizations. They are external lecturers at Roskilde University, Denmark, and they write books and articles on organizational psychology. Their website can be found at www.bonnerup-hasselager.dk.

Love and Loneliness at Work

An Inspirational Guide for Consultants, Leaders and Other Professionals

Birgitte Bonnerup and
Annemette Hasselager

LONDON AND NEW YORK

First published 2019
by Routledge
2 Park Square, Milton Park, Abingdon, Oxon OX14 4RN

and by Routledge
52 Vanderbilt Avenue, New York, NY 10017

Routledge is an imprint of the Taylor & Francis Group, an informa business

© 2019 Birgitte Bonnerup and Annemette Hasselager

The right of Birgitte Bonnerup and Annemette Hasselager to be identified as authors of this work has been asserted by them in accordance with sections 77 and 78 of the Copyright, Designs and Patents Act 1988.

All rights reserved. No part of this book may be reprinted or reproduced or utilised in any form or by any electronic, mechanical, or other means, now known or hereafter invented, including photocopying and recording, or in any information storage or retrieval system, without permission in writing from the publishers.

Trademark notice: Product or corporate names may be trademarks or registered trademarks, and are used only for identification and explanation without intent to infringe.

British Library Cataloguing-in-Publication Data
A catalogue record for this book is available from the British Library

Library of Congress Cataloging-in-Publication Data
Names: Bonnerup, Birgitte, author. | Hasselager, Annemette, author.
Title: Love and loneliness at work : an inspirational guide for consultants, leaders and other professionals / Birgitte Bonnerup and Annemette Hasselager.
Description: 1 Edition. | New York : Routledge, 2019. |
Includes bibliographical references and index.
Identifiers: LCCN 2018060080 (print) | LCCN 2019009306 (ebook) |
ISBN 9780429456220 (Master eBook) | ISBN 9780429851094 (Adobe Reader) |
ISBN 9780429851070 (Mobipocket) | ISBN 9780429851087 (ePub) |
ISBN 9781138315624 (hardback) | ISBN 9781138315631 (pbk.) |
ISBN 9780429456220 (ebk)
Subjects: LCSH: Work environment--Psychological aspects. | Loneliness. | Love.
Classification: LCC HF5548.8 (ebook) | LCC HF5548.8 .B646 2019 (print) |
DDC 658.3/14--dc23
LC record available at https://lccn.loc.gov/2018060080

ISBN: 978-1-138-31562-4 (hbk)
ISBN: 978-1-138-31563-1 (pbk)
ISBN: 978-0-429-45622-0 (ebk)

Typeset in Times New Roman
by Taylor & Francis Books
Printed by CPI Group (UK) Ltd, Croydon CR0 4YY

Contents

	Introduction	ix
1	Love and loneliness at Food for Fridays	1
2	Love	10

Why love? 10
Love in working life 12
Libido – love as a vital drive 13
Love as an active outwardly directed emotion 15
Love as the capacity to show tenderness and tolerate ambivalence 15
The love relationship as fusion and as differentiation 17
Love and projective and perceptive identification 19
Self-love 22
Love as a creative force 23
Love and the pair in the organization 24
The psychology of friendship and collusion as relational dynamics 26
Friendship 26
The psychology of friendship 28
Collusion 29
Pairs in working life 33
The libido is invested in the task 35
Ted and Arnie 35
The libido is invested in the relationship 37
The libido is directed at what the pair create together 39
The pair as group dynamic 42
The pair that others see 45
Love of the task 46

Love in the organization 58
Love of the group and the organization 59
The leadership team at Old Mill School 61
The libidinal centre 62
Closing remarks 64

3 Loneliness — 67

The phenomenon of loneliness 68
Loneliness and 'homo sentimentalis' 69
Positive thinking and loneliness 71
Everyday setbacks 73
Being someone 'special' 73
Loneliness in the workplace 74
Psychological concepts for understanding loneliness 77
Discrepancy between inner self and outer self 90
The changeling – feeling different 91
The trio – loneliness as a third wheel 100
Loneliness as group dynamic 102
Closing remarks 111

4 Theory — 115

The unconscious – a key concept in psychoanalysis 115
Anxiety 125
Libido 130
Projection, projective and perceptive identification 134
The inner and outer self 139

Index — 146

Introduction

Love and loneliness, in both their presence and absence, are key aspects of our lives – including our working lives. This is a book about our working life and about emotions in working life, including both the emotions that are difficult to handle and the ones that make it worthwhile for us to go to work, keep at it, seek to improve conditions, overcome difficulties, laugh and cry, struggle and strive.

Love and loneliness are concepts that have seized our interest for a variety of reasons. Loneliness is a persistent theme. We encounter loneliness in heads of departments, teachers, lawyers, doctors, expats, school directors, CEOs, consultants and many others. Although they are surrounded by others in many ways, many people feel lonely in one sense or another. This loneliness may be perceived as more or less vague. It may be experienced and expressed tacitly, go unmentioned or be taboo. Loneliness may be perceived as momentary or monumental.

Just as we encounter loneliness, we also encounter love in our working life. We are convinced – and we believe that others share this view – that it matters whether we like our co-workers, that it matters whether we like our tasks, the organization or our working life. To our knowledge, this aspect is less well documented in psychodynamic theory, where it is more common to find descriptions, for example, of anxiety, aggression and rivalry. Love involves empathy, care and tenderness. It involves responsibility, determination and persistence – and it involves joy, sorrow, anxiety, aggression, rivalry – of course. Love wants something, and it comes at a cost, and it is this dynamic that we want to address.

We have pulled Freud's concept of libido out from our mental bookshelves, where it has been gathering dust for a few years. Our reading and rereading of some of Freud's texts, insights and inspiration from Winnicott and new ideas from Bollas are the theoretical cornerstones of the present book. We invite the reader into the psychodynamic and psychoanalytic universe and perspectives on working life. In writing the present book, our goal has been to make it accessible to readers who do not necessarily have in-depth knowledge of the theoretical field and inspiring to readers who do. Some of our theoretical observations and ideas have undergone fairly careful consideration and are widely shared in psychodynamic organizational psychology. Others are more tentative and open, and we invite others to join us in considering and developing these ideas and concepts further.

The present book is one that invites reflection. Our hope is to offer inspiration and knowledge in order to enrich, challenge and bring meaning to working life. We are not going to translate the ideas in the book into guidelines for practice, as that would run the risk of becoming didactic, simplistic and normative. We hope to inspire our readers to reflect on and talk about working life, the choices we make and to care for the communities that exist. To think about what loneliness means in working life and about the pleasure of doing something one excels at, the pleasure of spreading one's wings and connecting with others.

We present a number of constructed cases that are not references to one specific person, group or organization, but a generalization and simplification of real-life phenomena. Our cases rewrite our collated experiences. Throughout the book, we use the cases to illustrate and discuss what is happening and could be happening in working life.

The content of the book

The book consists of four chapters. Chapter One is 'Food for Fridays', a story of love and loneliness in a Danish–Italian food import company. We meet the inhabitants of the company and follow the start-up phase and some of the company's happy moments and challenges. Although we refer to this story, and the characters in it, in the following chapters, it is not necessary to read it first. But it might be fun! Chapter Two is the main chapter on love. We explain why we find love such a relevant concept, and how we understand love from a psychodynamic perspective. We write about couples in the workplace and demonstrate the central role of the couple. We write about love of the task and of the organization. Chapter Three is the main chapter on loneliness. We demonstrate how loneliness can be understood in a sociological context, and how loneliness can be understood from the perspective of individual psychology. We introduce a distinction between loneliness and being alone and present the concepts of inner self and outer self. Based on real-life practice, we examine the experience of being lonely as it may appear in the form of the fear of exposure or of feeling out of place and excluded. We look at loneliness associated with a given role, focusing especially on the leader's loneliness, and we look at loneliness as a group dynamic. The fourth and final chapter of the book focuses on theory and consists of five sections, each providing a theoretical discussion of a key theme: the unconscious; anxiety; libido; projection and projective and perceptive identification; and the concepts of the inner self and the outer self, which are inspired by Winnicott's concepts of the true self versus the false self.

Writing this book has been fun, difficult, demanding, educational and frustrating but never trivial. Above all: we wrote it because we really couldn't help ourselves.

Chapter 1

Love and loneliness at Food for Fridays

In summer 1978, lightning strikes in Vittorio's life. Vittorio is Italian. He lives where he has always lived, with his family, as the beloved eldest son of Marco and Bianca, both of whom missed him desperately while he was away in Milan studying to become an agronomist. Thankfully he returned home and joined the family business. That is, until lightning struck. Lightning in the form of Laura, a leggy, curly-headed blonde from Denmark. Vittorio fell head over heels in love with the neighbour's Danish au-pair. He was so smitten that he joined her in Denmark when her time as an au-pair was up, and they had four children in rapid succession, the first before they even got married. No big deal. Times were changing, in Denmark those sorts of formalities were of little significance, they were in love, and Vittorio would do anything to make the leggy, curly-headed blonde happy. Even if it meant walking to the moon and back on crutches. What he did do was found a company: Food for Fridays, which combined his own passion for food and business with a way to provide for his family, as any man should, in Vittorio's opinion, women's lib and topless sunbathing notwithstanding.

Based on his love of Italian food and his knowledge of quality produce and agricultural production, he and Laura began to import food from Italy. Initially, they focused on products from his home region in Italy, which he sold to restaurants. That went surprisingly well. His little kitchen-table business turned a nice profit in its first year, Vittorio was encouraged and soon established an official office in the city. A particular point in his favour was that he was among the first to spot the business potential in organic food and sustainable production methods. A growing general focus on food, organic living, health and quality produce provided good growth conditions for Food for Fridays, and Vittorio knew how to make the most of this opportunity.

Vittorio was business-savvy, and back in Italy, his mama used her powers of persuasion and insistent charm to make good deals in the local area for the delivery of quality food products from his home region to Copenhagen, soon also to the greater North Zealand region and, in a few years' time, to much of Scandinavia. It was a huge undertaking, and Vittorio spent many hours working; perhaps too many hours. He often stayed up late, working at the kitchen table, after the rest of the family had gone to bed. In that situation, he loved his company, his order book, keeping his customers happy – and willing them to order a little more. He loved the sight of a full order book and seeing the money roll in at a steady rate, and the company was growing faster than their four children. In some ways, it was almost easier and more rewarding to run the company than to be a father and a husband. Back in Italy, mama was worried: 'You work too much, you'll be a dull husband, you'll die young, you'll get cancer because you're always working,' she would tell him when they met in Italy. Eventually, Laura was fed up with the long hours and the short fuse that was also part of the package. Vittorio was quick to anger. After a long, serious conversation late one night, Vittorio realized that it was not just a possibility but an absolute necessity to find some partners for the company, partners to share the responsibility and the workload.

Vittorio knew Carl from the business, trusted him, liked his personality, which in many ways complemented Vittorio's dynamic but also quick-tempered and emotional style with a solid, down-to-earth demeanour that Vittorio found both fascinating and sometimes annoying. Rita became the third partner: systematic and phlegmatic, she not only excelled at accounting and budgeting but also had good business sense and was a strong and reliable worker. There was no way anyone would ever exhaust Rita's energy, Vittorio sometimes thought, wondering to himself what she did during her limited spare time. Vittorio, Carl and Rita made a good trio. The company grew even bigger, was consolidated and generated good earnings. Vittorio was a happier and more satisfied husband and father, and he was pleased in the knowledge that whatever happened, he had made sure he would always own at least a 52% share of the company. He was happy to share the responsibility and to exchange ideas, but he was not going to give up the final say. After all, he was the one who had founded the company and built it up.

By spring 2006, the outlook was less optimistic. Vittorio, Rita, Carl and the employees of Food for Fridays all saw the way things were going. It was clear to anyone that the market for quality food was getting crowded, which was eating into both their turnover and their profits. Although they had a well-established market position, they were aware of the need to expand. Vittorio sometimes missed his early start-up days, when he still worked at the kitchen table, knew every detail of his business and saw a direct link between orders and earnings. Things were getting a little boring, and thus, for a variety of reasons it was time to come up with something new.

Whether it was really new, was debatable. But to Food for Fridays it was new. They decided to get into importing organic quality wines from Italy – where else?

Since none of them knew much about wine or the wine business, they chose to hire Ethan, a young man of only 24, whom Vittorio had a good feeling about. They had met while Ethan was working in a competing company, and now Vittorio saw a chance to both weaken his competitor and add a good employee to his staff. Ethan's condition was that he was made partner right away. No trial period, no requirement of earning the privilege. Partner or nothing. Vittorio saw the demand as a reflection of Ethan's business savvy and confidence, while Carl and Rita saw it as manipulation and an inflated ego. They were both annoyed that this upstart, who had no share in the making the company what it was today was made partner just like that. But he was. As with so many other issues, Vittorio had his way.

Ethan worked very hard for the first few years. He knew from the outset that it was going to be an uphill slog and a tough nut to crack, to establish Food for Fridays on the Danish wine market, but he liked the freedom and the courage he received from Vittorio and Food for Fridays. Moreover, he had felt flattered by Vittorio's offer, by the trust he was shown. A tough but also an exciting challenge. He was well aware that it was a market with many suppliers and a tough competition on price. The company's ambition was not, after all, to be the leading supplier for Mr and Mrs Jones's everyday habit; they would leave that to the supermarket chains. Their focus was on quality organic wine. A niche market with a limited supply, and even the most passionate eco-enthusiasts were not going to put up with sour-tasting wine at elevated prices. Ethan was sure it would work out; although he was young in years, he had experience, contacts and a nose for wine. However, after a few years of negative earnings he was less confident. Was it really a good business? And was Italy – hand on heart – really the best country for organic wine production? Food for Fridays was under pressure from New Zealand wine growers who had both capacity and experience in their favour.

Ethan thought about suggesting importing New Zealand wines. Strictly speaking, it was not written in stone that Food for Fridays could only import Italian products. But for some reason he never seemed to get around to raising the issue at the management meetings. It would be like suggesting installing urinals in a nunnery. Unthinkable. The wine import was struggling to get off the ground. The competition was cut-throat, and even though Ethan and the staff he had built worked hard, for the first few years they took losses. Ethan took it up with Vittorio, who encouraged him to keep pushing. Vittorio tried to reassure him that the company was well situated to handle the losses, and that he, Vittorio, appreciated Ethan's efforts. In recent years, the situation had improved slightly, but Ethan felt bad about not being able to deliver a better result. It began to eat at him; he felt that he was unsuccessful at work, that in contrast to the good story that Food for Fridays had always been, he was deadweight, a non-contributor. He felt all alone with his worries, and when he was in a particularly dark mood, he felt that he did not deserve his generous salary or his share in the annual profits. He tried repeatedly to bring up his concerns at the management meetings, but he could never get through to the others. It was as if they could not and would not hear his point. When her mood was particularly sour, Rita would more than suggest that Ethan was a drain to the rest of the team and to the company. Although Vittorio tried to admonish her, Ethan was left with a growing sense of loneliness.

A few years after Ethan had joined the company, Fabio joined the management team. Fabio was Vittorio's eldest son, and he and Ethan were almost the same age. Fabio and Ethan became friends. The age difference was negligible, they loved going out together, and Fabio's cheerful demeanour and high energy was contagious. Fabio put Ethan's worries about the wine import into a more realistic perspective. 'There's plenty of money,' Fabio might say, 'and with your nose for wine, we'll crack that market wide open, just look at all those families in the posh part of town – they're going to want organic wine, it's a no-brainer.' Without saying so directly, Fabio was aware that Ethan was a good friend because he was stable and reliable, and because his calm demeanour and his ability to stay true to one woman were abilities Fabio could admire, although he could never match them. Ethan's relationship with Carl and Rita was less personal. And after all, he could understand it if his close relationship with Vittorio and Fabio – and, in fact, with the rest of the Italian–Danish family – might spark jealousy.

Fabio was very interested in the company, but he was not that keen on having a management role. He possessed his father's infectious mood and his energetic and vivacious personality, and he was great at connecting with suppliers and business partners. It was hard not to like Fabio. Fabio certainly thought so. Food for Fridays needed Fabio's many connections and his ability to develop loyal suppliers. A few years after Ethan and Fabio had joined the management team, mama had passed away at a ripe old age, and Vittorio's father soon followed. The death of Vittorio's parents meant that Food for Fridays was at risk of losing its best and most important suppliers, unless someone else could take over the task of developing and maintaining contacts and agreements in Italy. Fabio took over, and he did an excellent job. The others just had to put up with the fact that he came and went as he pleased, that he might lack focus during management meetings, paying more attention to text messages, Twitter and Instagram, and that he was reluctant to get involved in difficulties in the company that were not directly related to him and his area of responsibility. Fabio built connections and maintained relations – an indispensable role – but management was not his strong suit.

Fabio and Ethan suggested to Vittorio and the other two partners that they hire a marketing and communication manager to take care of the large and growing task of marketing, e-commerce and communication via social media. They knew Catherine personally, a smart and responsible woman with excellent skills in this field. Catherine was hired and did her best in her position.

Viewed from the outside, and judged by the business results, most things in the company were going pretty well at this point, despite a difficult market. What was not going well at all was the management meetings. It was very difficult to make the management team and the meetings function. When they met, it felt as if all the energy had been sucked out the room. Inefficient and demoralizing. Boring, a waste of time, like dancing in molten tar. This is how Ethan experienced the meetings: Fabio was often a little late. If the mood was tense, or things got difficult, Vittorio would make rash decisions that were not quite clear to the others. As if he mostly just wanted to get out of there, escape the difficult situation. There is no doubt that Vittorio was committed, but he was not being very professional. Carl did not say much, he had grown terse and withdrawn in recent years, and Ethan found it increasingly difficult to see how Carl contributed – or that he was earning his keep. It was beginning to grate on Ethan. Rita could be emotional and erratic. Some days she would align herself with Vittorio's opinions in an almost kittenish way; on other occasions, she was feisty and sometimes rude and simplistic in her assessments. Her ire was mostly directed at Catherine, occasionally at Carl and never at Fabio. Initially, it was not directed at Ethan either, but later, he too felt her wrath. Catherine was loyal to the core, stable, hardworking, reliable. However, Ethan knew from Fabio that she was beginning to complain to him that she did not feel she was being appreciated in the same way as the others. An accurate observation.

In 2010, the men's lifestyle magazine *Manly* came out with a theme issue on men and food, with a special focus on the meeting of Italy and Scandinavia. Food for Fridays featured prominently in the issue and even made the front page. The portrait highlighted Fabio as the future CEO of Food for Fridays. The coverage was excellent, the advertising effect was priceless, and there were mouth-watering pictures of the food – in fact, of Fabio too, who looked pretty good in the stylish photos. Ethan was not blind to the fact that the article might spark both jealousy and irritation, but what he did not get was why Vittorio, who was normally so proud of his son, had never mentioned the article with a single word; nor had Fabio. It was Laura, Fabio's mother, who had shown Ethan the article. She was proud and showed it to everyone she talked to.

Based on the article, Food for Fridays had contacted another company for the delivery of high-quality gift baskets with Italian delicacies and organic wine, and later the new client had asked whether Food for Fridays would be able to deliver products to their canteen. This was a new area for Food for Fridays, which so far had focused on retail, but they decided to give it a chance. The article in *Manly* had led directly to this opportunity, and it turned out that Catherine's sense of new trends and Ethan's flair for quality wine and food combined to enable Food for Fridays to add yet another strong business area to the company's portfolio.

Vittorio was pushing 60, and the company, in its current construction was nearing its 30th anniversary. Vittorio had decided to celebrate the event as 'the 90-year birthday.' Without giving anyone a heads-up, he was also planning to announce the order of succession in the company. It would come as no surprise to anyone that he was going to put his first-born son at the helm of the company and make himself the head of the board. However, his plan to make Ethan an equal director, with a 25% ownership share, that would probably come as a surprise.

Vittorio's 60th birthday would mark a generational change at Food for Fridays. In a mix of melancholy, forethought and competitiveness, Vittorio had decided to hold a leadership development day facilitated by an external consultant. One of his business associates had recommended it, and Vittorio did not want to appear backwards; if his friends were embracing the modern times and holding leadership development seminars, Food for Fridays would follow suit. Maybe he also thought that it would be nice to have a day where everyone had the opportunity to express how grateful and delighted they were to be part of the management team at Food for Fridays.

At the consultant's suggestion, each member of the management was to prepare for the seminar by writing a speech to Vittorio, as if it were a speech they would give at his birthday party. The speech would be used at the seminar to reflect on Food for Fridays, the management task and the internal cooperation in the team. The speech had to include a personal assessment and observations on the joys and sorrows associated with working at Food for Fridays.

It is now the weekend before the seminar, and the members of the management team are preparing their speeches.

Ethan sits in his study at home. His wife and three kids have gone to the public swimming pool, so he has a couple of hours to himself to prepare. But he is at a loss. It is a strange assignment. He looks at the blank sheet of paper. The empty screen. He has long been thinking about changing jobs, going into business for himself. He has put out some feelers, it could work. On the other hand, Food for Fridays was still a great place to work with strong personalities and room to express them. He and Fabio have had a good working relationship for many years. As different as night and day – yet similar. Fabio, the ladies' man, with a string of affairs; Ethan, married to his high school sweetheart. Fabio is charming, he could sell sand in the Sahara and bottles of chlorinated water in a swimming pool. Ethan has a nose for business, timing, deals – he is good at making others shine and feel good. But he is always second to Fabio. And a little tired of playing second fiddle. He loves working with Fabio – and he hates it. The management meetings – that is a separate story: every single meeting is a mix of boring discussions about details, people showing up late, complete stagnation. Whenever Ethan argues in favour of something, Vittorio will look at him – and then often proceed to make the opposite decision of what Ethan is advocating. The pattern is becoming so settled that Ethan is able to have his way simply by arguing for the opposite of what he really wants. He cannot possibly bring any of that up at the seminar, but Ethan is confused. Why does his friendship with Fabio sometimes feel like animosity? Ethan feels that Fabio is too old to come and go as he pleases. It's all fine being man of the hour in *Manly*, but Food for Fridays is a workplace. The youthful charm will eventually fade, he ought to grow up and take responsibility for the business and all the employees who rely on Food for Fridays. What he might be able to address at the seminar is his relationship with Vittorio. He still feels a deep sense of gratitude to Vittorio, who is almost like a second father to him. Someone who believed in Ethan and never stopped believing in him, despite the setbacks. In recent years, though, his relationship with Vittorio has become less important than his relationship with the other managers. Ethan peeks again at an email with an offer of a very lucrative deal on a large consignment of wine from New Zealand, a basis for starting his own company, a good deal for Food for Fridays?

Fabio has a hangover. Just said goodbye to the flavour of the week. Sweet girl, maybe it's time to settle down and raise a family? Mom would be pleased, and he was not going to stay young forever. Sitting with his feet on the coffee table and his Mac in his lap. Bloody h…, what is he going to write? He considers being ruthlessly honest. Pointing out that Ethan is becoming a bit of a problem. A pedantic stick-in-the-mud. They had been a good team in the early years, when Ethan had more guts, and before he took a BA in Organization and became all structured and dull. Ethan tends to forget that his kind is ten a penny, whereas he, Fabio, is unique. Indispensable to the company. Client relations was not all fun and games, and frankly speaking, maybe Ethan was simply jealous of his opportunities? Of the cool article in *Manly*? Of his ability to drum up new business – and, sure, new women? By the way, he was thoroughly fed up with the other directors and especially with the meetings in the management team. They were largely a waste of time, and he mostly showed up to give Vittorio peace of mind. When it was his turn, the meetings would be different. They would all be conducted standing up, limited to 30 minutes max, and all decisions would have to be made on the spot. Maybe it was time for Rita and Carl to think about early retirement? He decides to improvise at the seminar, preparation is a waste of time, seminars are a waste of time. He gets up and makes himself an espresso in the kitchen.

Catherine has sat down in a café to do her writing. She has reserved the evening to write the text for the seminar, an assignment from some clever consultant. Difficult. Catherine is scared. Scared of losing her job, scared of not speaking up enough at the management meetings, scared of speaking up too much. The other day she had overheard Carl speaking to Rita referring to Catherine as 'the angora stalker.' Not funny. She is thinking about looking for another job, does not feel that her qualifications are being appreciated. She was asked to join Food for Fridays because she was good at marketing and communication. And frankly – if she had not been on her toes they would never have begun delivering gift baskets, let alone canteen food. It was not her idea, but she was instrumental in making the deal possible. The stable player who made the clients feel confident in picking Food for Fridays as a supplier of quality products. Shortly, she is going to write about how exciting it is to be part of the team at Food for Fridays, so the others can see how much she has to offer when they finally listen for once. Catherine is looking for a good opening line.

Rita. Has sat down at her desk after a good dinner at Robert's, her great love. Rita has found love late in life. That is none of the others' business. But maybe she is going to want to work less? Maybe she will want to travel more. She feels happy and alive. Food for Fridays is no longer the only important thing in her life. She wants to get home in the evenings, home to fun conversations about art, cross-country skiing and good red wine, not organic, not Italian, but still good wine. She is happy. She often thinks of the article in *Manly*. It had been helpful, it had led to good, new clients, a new business area. But something had happened. Vittorio had never mentioned the article; she is wondering what it was the article had started. Surely, it could not be something as trivial as envy of his own son, envy over not being the front man? The handsome young lion? Rita had trouble believing that was it. She had always been fond of Vittorio, with all his ideas, his warm personality, his genuine interest in many aspects of food and wine. She had also often wondered why she was not attracted to him. Was it possible that she was in love with Vittorio without being willing to see it? But she was not. She sincerely cared for him, but she was not attracted to him. Nothing like what she feels now. No comparison. Rita does not really care. It is nice to feel less absorbed in Food for Fridays, it is nice to want to take time off, not to want to check emails and phone messages when she is not at work. She wants to continue working for another ten years, wants to do the responsible thing. She knows she is good and virtually indispensable to the company. But it really is strange that Vittorio had never mentioned the article. The idea of writing a speech is a non-starter ... she would open with that. And that is all she would write. That is a discussion they would have to take at the seminar.

Carl was sitting comfortably in his sofa with a glass of cold ale within reach. Most of all he felt like opening with an announcement: I have been a life-long alcoholic, and none of you have noticed. Excessive drinking and hangovers, hidden behind a wall of silence. He had managed to limit drinking binges to holidays and weekends and stick to 'more than enough' on weekdays, enough to collapse on the sofa every evening, have poor and fitful sleep, and then, after a shower and in a freshly ironed shirt, being able to recover enough to seem merely introvert and quiet. He had fit in, wanted it that way. A good and long friendship with Vittorio and maybe also with Rita. But based on what? Vittorio was a savvy businessman, but a really poor judge of character. Carl also had concerns for the future. With Fabio as the new CEO, which was to be expected – what would that be like? Would he be regarded as part of the threadbare furnishings, something to get chucked out when Vittorio was no longer at the helm? Carl drifted off, took a sip of his beer, wanted to keep it safe. Describing how pleased he was to be part of the team, all the personalities with all their differences, who complemented and brought the best out in each other, ups and down – mostly ups. A huge success and a great place to work. Keen to do another lap, another ten years. Yes, something along those lines. Hot air, sure. But necessary.

It might be interesting to see how the seminar proceeds. Will they manage to speak about any of the important issues, will they find the courage to develop Food for Fridays together, or are they just going to pass the time as best they can, until the seminar is over, without too many bruises?

It might also be interesting to take part in the 90-year birthday. If nothing else, there would probably be good food and ample amounts of good wine. It might be interesting to be present when Vittorio announces his plans for the future ownership. What is Fabio going to say – and is Ethan going to want to stay? Whether Food for Fridays survives the generational change, and whether Fabio decides to grow up might also be interesting to know. But then, as Food for Fridays does not exist, it's really up to you.

Chapter 2

Love

Why love?

Why focus on love in working life? Can love even be a relevant, useful or necessary concept in an organizational context? Even though we do not deal with romantic love, but with love in everyday working life, we will address this question first. In both its presence and its absence, the love we examine in this book is a commonplace experience for many people in postmodern working life who find that work offers opportunities for entering into meaningful and important relationships. That, by offering an outlet for engagement and competence and by providing an opportunity for making a difference, work lets us experience love of our work tasks. That when we are given, and seize, the opportunity to develop good relationships with our co-workers and the organization, we have a strong impact on our individual quality of life, the quality of our work and our abilities to overcome problems, conflicts and other challenges together. That for many, working life can become a source of profound and lasting friendships. And that our attachment to our workplace is a key source of meaning for many of us. That is the kind of love we aim to examine and unfold, and those are the aspects that the concept of love in a working life context is going to help us understand.

There is a certain reluctance associated with writing about love. A sense of vulnerability. Although it is an everyday experience for many – including ourselves – we prefer being with certain people, that some working relationships are more exciting to be a part of than others, and that there are certain organizational contexts we gladly prioritize over others. These are not necessarily simpler but loving relations, where difficult tasks and challenging times are easier to handle because those involved like each other and invest sufficient interest and energy in each other and in handling the difficulties. Uncomplicated relations can also be dull relations, where nothing is at stake, neither the quality of the work effort nor of the relationship itself. The reluctance pertains to the challenge of identifying, defining, articulating something that is commonplace, yet is still so undefinable that it can only be fully captured by poets and composers. And so much has been written, conceived, sung and spoken about love.

This made us wonder. It seems to be easier to criticize than to show affection. Easier to identify flaws and inadequacies than possibilities. Why is that? And why is it, apparently, easier to write about aggression, anxiety and destruction than about love? Perhaps toward the end of the chapter, we can offer the beginnings of an answer to these questions. First, we need to address the concept of love. What are we talking about when we talk about love?

Over the past century, numerous practical and theoretical contributions have suggested how we can use psychological insights to understand and enhance the development of working life. With these insights we have achieved greater nuance and depth in our understanding of the psychology of leadership and management, cooperation, group dynamics and the psychology of change processes, among other aspects. For good and bad, psychology has become a factor in our understanding of work, cooperation, leadership and management and of the practical performance of work tasks. Our main focus in the present context is on relations at work and how we care for and engage with each other and our work tasks.

We are interested in the potential that lies in caring for important workplace relations; in treating them as an important resource, a necessity for the employees and for job performance. For example, if we consider the wider issue of well-being, the focus often deals with the well-being of *the individual*. In a publication from the Danish Health Authority, for example, it reads, 'The future effort for health and well-being in the workplace should ensure that employees get healthier from going to work than they would if they stayed at home. The vision is that in the future, working life is going to make a 'positive contribution to the citizens' health' (Sundhedsstyrelsen, 2009; (Danish Health Authority) our translation). Here, the emphasis is clearly on individual well-being, on what the workplace should *ensure* or *contribute* or *provide* with relation to the employee, who, in a manner of speaking, can simply show up and expect to receive these benefits. In our opinion, there is good reason to focus on what the individual can provide and contribute to the group – rather than what the individual more or less passively expects to receive – and to examine the potential of enabling individuals to opt in, rather than opting out for the purpose of self-protection. We should consider what interpersonal relationships mean for group well-being and work performance. What if some of the many people suffering from stress are not merely stressed by their workload, contradictory demands, impossible deadlines and pointless routines? We have long known that good working relationships offer protection against stress – maybe, conversely, the disruption of good working relationships can even be a cause of the stress?

Love in working life is also a condition for having the trust, determination, courage and desire to make it through difficult times: times characterized by relational problems, task-related difficulties, work tasks that seem impossible, organizational mergers and break-ups, challenging market conditions and so forth. We believe that having a loving relationship with others, with the task and with the organization improves one's capacity to overcome difficulties – including difficulties related to output, efficiency, economics and the bottom line.

However, it is no simple matter to invite the concept of love into the context of organizational psychology. Love is probably one of the most revisited themes in popular literature, B-films and pop music as well as in more serious literature and art. Love is a concept steeped in clichés and preconceived notions (cf. Gadamer's concept of prejudice (Højbjerg, 2005)). Some would argue that love is a strictly private matter, and any attempt at bringing it into a workplace context might be seen as yet another attempt at colonizing the psyche and soul. There are many good reasons to think twice before taking on this difficult task. However, in a sense, these reservations also present an important argument for continuing our quest. From our perspective, love plays a role – and an important role – in many spheres of life and in a wide range of human relationships. That includes working life.

Love is inherently easy to experience but difficult to define. We feel greater warmth, tolerance and interest toward some people than others. Love is a complex emotion, and in loving relations we experience many different basic emotions, not merely positive ones but the entire range of emotions. Love makes it possible to bear, examine and discard certain types of negative emotions, develop positive emotions, carry on and develop shared experiences and a shared history, which may potentially, but not necessarily, enhance the degree of love in the relationship. Love can develop and grow stronger over time; an experience that many will recognize. However, even brief relationships, for example a collaboration in connection with a work task of limited duration, can also be driven by profound feelings of love.

In the following, we seek first to define love as a concept that we can incorporate and use. Next, we seek to define and describe love in working life as a phenomenon in interpersonal relations, with relation to the work tasks we engage in, in groups and in the relationship between the individual and the organization they are a part of. We argue that it makes a difference whether we like and care for the people we work with.

Love in working life

Love is said to follow its own unfathomable path and perhaps its very essence is equally beyond our understanding. So where to turn, if we wish to determine what love is and what it means in working life? Our interest in the present context is limited to how psychology defines and understands love, although we are well aware that psychology does not, by any stretch of the imagination, have a monopoly on this crucial phenomenon.

In psychology, the theoretical framework of psychoanalysis and the psychodynamic tradition offers insight into what may seem incomprehensible. Question such as, why do we not always act in a way that would appear to be in our own best interest? Why do we do something other than what we intended? And why do we keep doing something that we promised ourselves and others we would stop doing? Psychoanalysis and the psychodynamic theories (thankfully) do not hold the final answer, but they can offer possible insights and explanations. We set out to investigate what psychoanalysis can tell us about the nature of love, the substance of love, the paths of love and – not least – the role of love in working life and organizations.

We have searched in vain for an overarching and complete theory of love within a psychoanalytic framework. Although Freud did write about love, his observations are scattered, not put together in a coherent treatise. Erich Fromm wrote the 1956 book *The art of loving*, a highly popular book, which is clearly influenced by the time of its writing. Otto Kernberg, who is a leading figure in modern psychoanalysis, also addressed the topic in his 1995 book *Love relations. Normality and pathology*, which focuses on personal love. French psychoanalysts, most notably Jacques Lacan (Demandante, 2014) and the philosopher Alain Badiou (2015), have also written about love. We are in fascinating company, with many different perspectives and many possibilities of getting lost. To pick a starting point, let us turn to Freud, the father of psychoanalysis.

Libido – love as a vital drive

One of the classic psychoanalytic concepts is the concept of libido. In recent years, it appears to have fallen slightly out of use. In psychodynamic organizational psychology, libido appears to have played a very limited role and has not been treated as a fundamental concept, perhaps because it is primarily associated with the sexual drives. In any circumstance, however, libido is a psychoanalytic concept that pertains to love, and hence, we will examine it here.

Like so many other Freudian concepts, Freud's concept of libido is nebulous. Throughout his writings, he continually altered the concept without, however, adjusting his previous models and theories. In his later drive theory, he defines libido as a set of vital drives. Love arises as a result of the vital drives, which seek the continuation of the species (sexual drives) and the preservation of life (self-preservation). We love the person who protects us from danger, provides nourishment, gives birth to children. Based on the definition of libido as a set of vital drives it became possible to define love as a more general phenomenon, expanding it to include creating or developing something. In *Group psychology and the analysis of the ego*, Freud addressed the libido as a vital drive. Here he writes,

> We are of opinion, then, that language has carried out an entirely justifiable piece of unification in creating the word 'love' with its numerous uses, and that we cannot do better than take it as the basis of our scientific discussions and expositions as well.
>
> (Freud, 1921/1955b, p. 90)

The concept of libido offers certain possible perspectives to facilitate our understanding of love. Libido is psychic energy, libido is transformed into engagement, attention, interest in the other, creative urges, nurture, desire. Libido is not body *or* psyche, volition *or* emotion, but rather a cocktail that comprises it all. Libido is physical tension, arousal and mental focus, determination, desire, emotional excitement, focused presence in the moment. Libido is decisions, perseverance, determination, joy and tenderness. Does that mean libido encompasses everything, one might ask? No, libido is not withdrawal, stagnation, complacency, exhaustion, defeatism, indifference, lethargy, sleep, relaxation. Libido is psychic energy directed at something or someone; libido has an object.

Freud often used metaphors from the world of physics. As such, libido can be understood as an electrical current that may switched be on or off, that may have higher or lower voltage and that may run in different directions. That metaphor alone does not fully capture the nature of libido, however. Libido can be difficult to restrain, libido can take off in many directions, chasing a specific object or a vague dream, libido can take many paths and easily gets in the way of the ego. Libido is like the unconscious – powerful, alive, inherently uncontrollable (although one gradually learns to control its expression, with varying degrees of success). Libido may offer part of the explanation why people have children, even in a society with old-age pensions and legalized abortion, libido may be the explanation why children build towers of toy bricks and then gleefully knock them down only to rebuild them. It explains countless spires, towers and ornamental decorations on buildings, all the effort that goes into maintaining relations with friends and family and the energy we invest in our work, our work assignments and our co-workers. The libido is difficult to restrain and expressing it can be a wonderful feeling.

Libido is a concept that describes internal psychological processes, but it is always directed at someone or something. Either internally, in the form of thoughts and emotions directed at ideas or notions about us and about certain others – or certain aspects of these others. Or directed at actual persons or tasks. Thus, libido can be directed at individual others as well as at an idea or an organization.

Libido is not stagnation. It is not passivity, absence and indifference. There is something at stake. An energy that seeks an expression and a reply. That seeks to find a path, even when that path may not exist. Libido meets the external world, and libido meets others' libido. Libido is a state of targeted energy. Libido can have multiple targets at once. We do not believe there is any particular reason to think of libido as a finite individual resource that might be used up, so to speak. It is also not sufficient to assume there is some sort of karmic law at play: that the more you give, the more you receive in return. It is not that simple. We will leave it to the following: libido meets the external world, and something happens.

Freud is often attributed with the notion that love and work are the two central elements of human life, and that mental health can be understood as having the opportunity to love and work. Erik Erikson writes that Freud 'is reported as to have' made such a statement, but it does not appear to be possible to find it in Freud's writings. Freud did, however, express a personal ambition of being married to Martha while also pursuing his work: 'Couldn't I for once have you and the work at the same time?' (Freud–Martha Bernays, 21 October 1885). We elaborate further on the concept of libido in the chapter on theory.

Love as an active outwardly directed emotion

Libido as a life drive is an element of a psychodynamic understanding of love. But what else can we find? Erich Fromm's 1956 book *The art of loving* gained a wide readership that went far beyond the psychoanalytic and psychological profession. Fromm was a psychologist and psychoanalyst, inspired by Freud and Marx, and one of the first representatives of what later became known as the Frankfurt School. Fromm writes, 'Love is an activity, not a passive affect; it is a "standing in," not a "falling for." (...) love is primarily giving, not receiving' (Fromm, 1956, p. 21). It is one of Fromm's key points that many want to be loved but are not sufficiently focused on loving. Love is an emotion with an external target, an activity that seeks someone or something outside the person.

That may sound like a pop song. But Fromm has a point. Love is attached to something or someone that receives the love and may reciprocate in some form or another. It is an important point that the other is not merely the receiver or the sender of projections; the other has a presence in their own right. We need to include 'the other' in our understanding. Love can be directed at a lofty ideal, a utopia, just as it may be directed at a specific and present work task, a baby, an incoming new manager, a former son-in-law and so forth. Initially, mainly as an imagined rather than a concrete libido cathexis. The relationship may subsequently develop, so that a shared history takes form. Fromm emphasizes the active character of love and underscores that certain basic elements are common to all forms of love: care, responsibility, respect and knowledge (ibid., p. 26). In a point that is highly relevant to the second theme of the present book, Fromm also defines 'separateness' as the main issues of the human condition and argues that love is the answer (ibid., p. 8).

Love as the capacity to show tenderness and tolerate ambivalence

The American psychoanalyst Otto Kernberg is probably best known for his work on narcissistic personalities. However, he is also the author of the interesting book *Love relations. Normality and pathology* (Kernberg, 1995). Although Kernberg's book deals with romantic love, not love in the broader meaning that we address here, some of his points are highly relevant to our context. In a love relationship, the parties will unconsciously connect with each other by identifying with certain qualities in each other and by attributing attractive and desirable as well as unwanted and less appealing traits to one another. It is part of the nature of the love relationship that both parties, so to speak, push psychological processes, elements and character traits back and forth between them. Other scholars besides Kernberg have described this pattern, including Jakobsen and Visholm (1987). It is not a question whether the pair is going to engage in this pattern or not; it emerges on its own. However, it can take different forms that may be more or less helpful for a healthy love relationship. Kernberg points out that through these projective processes the two parties care for each other but also risk locking each other into patterns that may be unhelpful. A love relationship has the best conditions to thrive if both parties are capable of a nuanced and realistic understanding, which involves the understanding that the other is not, for example, 'always grumpy' but is sometimes grumpy in a way that may be difficult or annoying, and that they do not always 'reject any new idea' but may perhaps possess a certain reluctance that is especially pronounced in certain situations (Kernberg, 1995).

With Kernberg, we can safely state that love relations are not simple, in case anybody was suffering under that delusion. The parties in a love relationship may well alternate between looking out for themselves or the other person, and both may, to varying degrees, experience being taken hostage by the other's psyche. The love relationship inevitably produces contradictory feelings about oneself as well as the other. That leads to ambivalence, and a mature love relationship requires an evolved capacity to accept this ambivalence without falling into a one-sided, generalized and simplistic view of oneself or the other.

Both parties invest libido in the other but also in joint ideas and dreams about what this particular pair can accomplish together: a wonderful child, a bridge, an especially delicious cake recipe and, not least, their perception of themselves as a pair and of what they can accomplish together: 'You and I can write a book together, a book that no one else could write.' Kernberg has an important point here. The pair also needs to invest libido in the notion of themselves as a pair. In other words, a pair contains three elements that the libido needs to be invested in: the two individuals and the pair as a unit.

Kernberg describes the ability to show and provide care as a prerequisite to establishing and maintaining a mature love relationship. The ability to provide care springs from the ability to feel and show tenderness. Kernberg describes how this capacity for tenderness develops during in the early, pregenital stage of life; that is, as a non-sexual phenomenon. In the mature love relationship, tenderness is expressed as tenderness for the other's vulnerability, eccentricities, imperfections and ambitions, for example tenderness toward the other's baffling desires and demands. That does not necessarily involve fulfilling these desires or demands; it simply means feeling and showing tenderness toward the fact that they exist. It is not important to reject their existence, nor is it important to go along. We have not seen other theorists highlight tenderness as an element of the concept of love, and in our opinion, Kernberg has an important point here. The inclusion of tenderness frames love as something directed at the other, who is, importantly, another in their own right. It also highlights the fact that love contains a wide range of different emotions directed at the other, in their own right, as being different from oneself.

With Freud, Fromm and Kernberg, we now have some important building blocks to help us build an understanding of love based on psychoanalytic and psychodynamic theory. Freud proposes libido as a conceptualization of the vital drives and demonstrates how libido can be invested in oneself and one's internal notions as well as in external objects – actual persons, ideas, things. Fromm shows us that love is an active feeling directed at someone or something, and that love also involves care, responsibility, respect and knowledge. We see that love comprises many different emotions – and that it comprises more than emotions. Kernberg underscores that love relations will always contain ambivalence, and that the capacity to contain this ambivalence is crucial. Furthermore, he points out that love is nourished by tenderness; tenderness that is directed lovingly at the other *as* the other.

The love relationship as fusion and as differentiation

As mentioned earlier, we choose to assign the psychoanalytic concept of libido a central position in our understanding of love. As described above, libido is invested in persons, tasks and objects in the real world as well as in our internal notions about them. Our discussion is framed by the assumption that we consider the external world to have an actual existence, at the same time as we assume that we can never perceive it 'as it really is.' Reality is understood and interpreted through our sensations, ideas and experiences. As some readers will be aware, this touches on a discussion about theory of science, which we will not, however, venture further into (interested readers may consult, e.g., Bonnerup & Hasselager, 2008, where this discussion is elaborated). However, in order to address and understand the following points about the psychological meaning of love, we need to remember that love as libidinous cathexis unfolds both in us and between us. Love unfolds internally, within us, as cathexis of self-concepts and cathexis of perceptions of (whole or partial) actual persons, relations, groups, workplaces, tasks and other phenomena. And love unfolds between us in the form of libido directed at real persons, relations, groups, workplaces, tasks and other phenomena.

Using the concepts of psychoanalysis, we can examine the love relationship as fusion and as differentiation. Or, to be more specific, as a relationship that may be dominated by either fusion or differentiation. When fusion dominates, we often speak of a symbiosis, with the mother–infant relationship as the most obvious example, both with relation to the child's concrete experience and as a basic concept in psychoanalytic developmental psychology. Symbiosis or fusion is characterized by the absence of a distinction between 'you' and 'me'; the boundaries between subject and object are fluid, vaguely defined or entirely absent. However, symbiosis far extends the early developmental stage in the human individuation process. It is also a form that adult love relationships may be defined by, draw on, borrow from or tend toward. The parties identify with one another, become and 'are' a whole, identical. Their perceived identity is associated with the whole, the pair, me-and-my-workplace, me-and-my-profession. Identification processes in symbiosis correspond to an elimination of differences and boundaries. I am the other, neither of us can tell ourselves apart.

When differentiation dominates, boundaries exist and are maintained. There is a difference between 'you' and 'me.' Maybe one appreciates a close co-worker, because they have desirable qualities that one lacks, and which one admires or maybe even envies. This represents a libidinal investment in something that is different from oneself. 'I want something the other has,' 'I want to be something the other is,' 'I copy and learn.' In their book *Freuds psykoanalyse* [Freud's psychoanalysis], Olsen and Køppe use the example of someone admiring Humphrey Bogart to elucidate the key difference between copying Humphrey Bogart (based on differentiation) and thinking that one is Humphrey Bogart (fusion) (Olsen & Køppe, 1981, p. 435).

This distinction contains certain obvious pitfalls. One is to view symbiosis as being more primitive, and differentiation as being more mature. In developmental terms, the former may precede the latter, but both are present at a very early stage in the child's life (Stern, 1985). We are not going to elaborate on developmental issues in the present context but merely wish to point out that in our view, the two types of relationships are – and should be – equally valuable. Symbiosis or identification is an important element in achieving and maintaining identity and belonging. We build group identity by highlighting internal similarities while positioning differences outside the 'we.' It is a common experience, for example in connection with joining a group, establishing a friendship or entering into a romantic relationship, that the similarities between the parties are emphasized, articulated and assessed as positive qualities, and that differences are positioned outside the group/the pair/the couple/the organization and are often attributed negative meaning. That phenomenon is well described in theoretical works (see, e.g., Dalal, 2002). Another pitfall is to see only the obvious truths: we are all different, every human being is unique and valuable in their own way, you have to be able to sense yourself and your personal boundaries to be able to enter into good relations with others. This is all true, but it is also quite superficial.

Fusion and differentiation can be regarded as concurrent psychological processes, both of which are part of and contribute to the love relationship with all the libidinal forms of cathexis. Neither can stand alone: too much fusion, and the individual disappears; too much differentiation, and the 'we' suffers. In our experience, however, the most difficult issue to deal with in love relations is differentiation. Differences are often felt to threaten the symbiosis, for good and bad, especially during the first stages of pairing and group life. This means that there are powerful forces at play in the drive for identification and the emphasis on similarities in the most important relationships in our life. It is worth examining and considering how love relations in working life can master both fusion and differentiation.

Love and projective and perceptive identification

Regarding the other with a tender gaze. That is how Winnicott describes the child's vital need to be mirrored in the mother's loving gaze and, later, the mother's need to see herself mirrored in the child's gaze. That requires symbiosis – 'we are one' – as well as differentiation – 'and yet, we are two.' The two individuals and the pair-as-unit. Here, we need to bring in three other fundamental concepts from psychoanalysis and psychodynamic psychology: projection, projective identification and perceptive identification. We will address them one at a time.

Projection has both an everyday meaning, referring to a basic psychological process, and a more narrow, specific meaning, referring to a psychological defence mechanism. In its general meaning, it describes a psychological process where we use the experience of our own body sensations and mental perceptions as a basis for recognizing ourselves and the other in the projection. We interpret and find meaning in others' actions and reactions and form ideas about their state of mind based on our own experiences, which we identify/recognize in the other, without fully forgetting that they are in fact our own. Projection is used as a defence mechanism in situations where the individual unconsciously extrudes something associated with internal distress, pain or anxiety by identifying the undesired aspects in and attributing them to another/others. Projective mechanisms – whether as a basic psychological process or as a defence mechanism – unfold in every domain of human life, including our working life. For example, many workplace managers are, from time to time, perceived as being harsh, insensitive and indifferent to their employees' well-being – qualities that are poorly aligned with the individual manager's own self-perception.

The psychoanalyst Melanie Klein formulated the so-called object relations theory, which is a further development of psychoanalysis that deviates from Freud's thinking in some regard. Her theory has had a major impact within clinical psychology and her ideas have also found their way into organizational psychology (see, e.g. Heinskou & Visholm, 2004). In the early 1950s, Klein coined the term 'projective identification,' which has since gained widespread use. It is a complicated concept, and there have been continuous theoretical discussions, for example about whether it describes internal individual processes (intrapsychological processes) or whether it captures psychological processes that unfold between people (interpersonal processes)

(Olsen, 2002). In the present context, we treat the concept as a strictly interpersonal phenomenon.

Defining projective identification as an interpersonal process became a particular focus for some of Klein's students at the Tavistock Institute in London. Projective identification is regarded as a special process that unfolds between mother and child, between client and therapist in psychotherapy and in social relations. The process of projective identification is often described as involving three steps: In step one, the projector or subject, unconsciously tries to extrude inner aspects (emotions, ideas) that are distressing, anxiety-provoking or unwanted. This corresponds to the process described above for projection. In step two, the recipient (the person who is in a relationship with the subject – for example the co-worker, the supervisor, the boyfriend/girlfriend or the therapist) to some extent identifies with the projected material and internalizes it, for example by feeling a particular emotion that the subject extruded. In step three, the recipient either rejects the projection, identifies with it or contains it and returns it to the subject at the appropriate time and place. Projective identification processes may unfold in different ways, sometimes fixating, some promoting development and change. The key point is the extent to which they represent a defence with or without reality orientation and how easy – or how difficult – it is for the parties in the projective relationship to examine and develop a more nuanced understanding of the projective processes. In the example above, which involved projective elements in the relationship between manager and staff, the outcome, in a simplified analysis, would hinge on whether the manager has a nuanced understanding of himself and the employees that enables him to understand why he is being perceived as harsh, uncaring and indifferent to the employees' well-being, and whether the employees understand why the manager may have to make decisions that have a negative impact on their working conditions.

Projection and projective identification are elements in any love relationship; both as ways of showing empathy with the other and as ways of connecting by attributing one's own qualities, emotions and motives into the other. The limitation of the concepts of projection and projective identification is that it is difficult to see that the love relationship is also a process that involves a libidinal investment in the other as an *other*, in the other's otherness, as someone different from oneself. Based on the work of object relations theorists (Klein and, especially, Winnicott, who built on and modified her theories), the English psychoanalyst Christopher Bollas has developed a range of concepts. Of these, his concept of perceptive identification is particularly interesting and relevant in the present context. Perceptive identification appears to have potential as a concept that addresses the limitation mentioned above.

Projective identification is a concept that concerns the individual's projections into the other. Bollas writes, 'a problem with the concept of projective identification is that it is not categorically interested in the object's qualities *per se*, but in the self's projections into the object (Bollas, 2007, p. 66). In

Bollas's understanding, the developmental phase that Klein labelled the depressive position is followed by a phase that Bollas calls 'object integrity,' where the child is able to perceive the object as something that has its own qualities, 'a thing in itself' (ibid.). In Bollas's terminology, the psychological process that the child develops during this phase is perceptive identification.

During the 'object integrity' phase, the child develops the ability to discover and acknowledge that the object (the other) has an independent existence. Perceptive identification includes perceiving the other's identity as distinct and different from one's own. Not by recognizing one's own emotions and perceptions in the other but by being aware of the other's different emotions and ideas and perceiving the difference as a quality of the relationship. This lets us see the other in their otherness, rather than as a mirror image of our own projections and phantasies. With this awareness, we can experience and enjoy the other's – the object's – qualities. This requires a separateness, a distinction, between subject and object and the capacity to perceive and enjoy the *difference* between subject and object (Bollas, 2007; Nettleton, 2017).

Perceptive identification is a relevant and obvious concept to include in our effort to unfold a psychoanalytic understanding of love. That is also one of Bollas's points. He writes, 'Perceptive identification allows us to love an object. A mature form of love, it does not function in accord with the intrinsically narcissistic axioms of projection and introjection … Rather than separateness and difference leading to emotional distance – as some might assume – such love creates the possibility for a wider range and a greater depth of intimacy with the object or other. By perceiving the object's features, the object is loved *for itself* not *for oneself*' (Bollas, 2007, p. 66).

Like projective identification, perceptive identification is a processual concept. Bollas argues that in our relations with others we vary between perceptive and projective identification (Bollas, 2007; Nettleton, 2017). With the concept of perceptive identification Bollas also underscores that there are two different forms of identification. In projective identification, *identification* means that the object identifies with the aspects that the subject extrudes in the projection process. In perceptive identification, identification means that the subject perceives the object's identity (Bollas, 2007, p. 68). Bollas underscores that developing one's capacity for perceptive identification is a condition for mature love relations (Nettleton, 2017, p. 49).

In a love relationship between self and object, we oscillate between projective identification and perceptive identification. This oscillation is crucial for the relationship. Perceptive identification lets one appreciate and relate to the other as distinct from oneself and as possessing their own integrity, and one is able to perceive the other's identity. Projective identification allows one to project part of oneself into the other and form ideas about their inner qualities, thoughts and emotions. Projection and projective identification are concepts and processes that are elaborated, approved and applicable in psychodynamic thinking. Perceptive identification is an important conceptual contribution to our effort to establish a definition and understanding of love that rests on a psychological and psychodynamic foundation, as it enables us to develop a psychoanalytically founded understanding of a key element of the love relationship: that the self relates to, perceives and experiences the object – the other – as separate and distinct, and that the perception and enjoyment of this difference is part of the love relationship.

Self-love

Our understanding of love must also include the ability to accept and appreciate oneself, to feel self-love. Many self-help and therapeutic approaches underscore that we have to be able to love ourselves before we can love anyone else. But what does that really mean, and what are the implications of it within the conceptual framework of the present book? In the chapter on loneliness we examine what the difference is between loneliness and being alone. We understand 'being alone' as the ability to be on one's own without feeling involuntarily excluded from relations with others. The ability to be on one's own depends in part on investing libido in one's inner notions and on what kind of inner notions the libido is invested in; it matters who one is with, when one is alone (Buechler, 2011), and it is important to be able to appreciate oneself and – remembering Kernberg – to regard oneself with tenderness and embrace ambivalent emotions.

The ability to invest libido in oneself is a key element of the ability to survive organizations and life in general. Regardless of good collegial relations, exciting work tasks and management's support, working life inevitably also includes failure, conditions we simply have to accept, decisions that do not turn out in our favour and unresolved or unresolvable conflicts. The ability to stand up for our own points of view, regardless of opposition and to handle and have the courage to enter into demanding relations with co-workers, clients, patients or citizens in turn depends on our ability to appreciate our own qualifications and to embrace ourselves with acceptance and tenderness. That includes having a realistic level of self-appreciation and regarding our own patterns and inadequacies with tenderness and tolerance – to be able to think, feel and self-correct: 'I guess my angry reaction just now was really over the top; I think I was being too touchy,' without feeling the need to rationalize or apologize. Self-appreciation is an individual experience. Being able to appreciate and love aspects of ourselves, so that, if nothing else, we are in good company when we are alone or have a good inner friend, whenever we encounter envy or invalidation.

The ego-ideal is part of the individual's psychological structure. Initially, Freud used the term 'ego-ideal' as an independent concept; later, he incorporated it as an aspect of the super-ego (Olsen, 2002; Freud 1921/1955b, pp. 65–144). In the present context, the ego-ideal is understood as the part of the super-ego that contains our ideal function: what the ego strives to realize and our individual norms for what is good, beautiful and right – the touchstone the ego uses for self-evaluation. The other part of the super-ego contains the conscience function: self-observation, self-criticism, dream censorship and repression barriers. The super-ego forms during childhood, modelled primarily on the child's parents. In adulthood, the ego-ideal continues to occupy a central position in the personality, but the content is detached from the actual persons who contributed to its formation. The ego-ideal – in combination with a certain degree of realism – can serve as the basis for strivings and desires to acquire knowledge and skills, learning, being something commendable, like an astronaut or a chef or a good father. When others affirm the ego-ideal, not in the form of projective processes but as perceptive identification, that contributes to a sense of worth and of love in the relationship. The other regards both the ego and the ego-ideal with libido and makes it even more valuable.

Love as a creative force

Love and love relations contain a creative force. In the case of romantic love, the couple bound up in the love relationship may create a child. Love relations in working life also have the potential to create something major, novel, special. That is obvious, of course, in artistic and creative fields, such as music, literature, architecture, design and media production. But it applies more broadly. It also includes the small, dedicated project team working on an innovation project to develop a new method for organizational learning; the teaching team preparing a new introduction to German grammar for the eighth form; the nursing team planning a Christmas event at a nursing home; or the scholar, absorbed in their work, putting together the elements for a new theory. In psychoanalytic terms, it happens whenever there is a libidinal investment in an endeavour and in the relations between the persons involved in creating something new. In such a working process, we might experience what Csikszentmihalyi (1990) calls *flow*, the concept he became known for during the 1990s, and what he defines as a mental state where one is completely involved in and focused on an activity. Flow is an experience that is charged with psychic energy, an absence of concern for the self, complete concentration and a sense of mastery of the task at hand (ibid.). Flow is conceptually rooted in positive psychology, but Csikszentmihalyi underscores that the phenomenon occurs when there is sufficient anxiety to keep us on our toes as well as sufficient security to prevent us from seizing up. This understanding is also found in learning concepts within psychodynamic organizational psychology (see, e.g., Visholm, 2001).

Thus, love as a creative force is love for the persons involved, for the future product of the activity and for the process itself. It is an important point that the opposite of love is not hate, conflicts, disagreement, sorrow or anger. Love contains complex emotions, and creative processes will almost always, inevitably, be fraught with difficulty, stress and conflict. The opposite of love as a creative force must be indifference. Indifference toward relationships, products and process cannot be creative.

Love and the pair in the organization

The pair as a basic figure

The concept of love is closely associated with the pair or couple. Pairs exist in real life and as inner representations based on our experiences and notions of pairs, specific pairs and the pair as figure. The pair is a basic psychological figure, where two pairs in particular emerge as central: the *mother–child couple* and the *romantic couple*. A third important couple or pair, which is less iconic but absolutely essential in life, is the *friendship pair*. Organizations are full of pairs. Formally and structurally defined pairs and pairs that emerge in the shared responsibility for a work task, all with their own unique psychology. In the following, we take a closer look at love and pairs in organizations and at the possibilities and challenges their presence gives rise to.

There are many different kinds of pairs in working life. There is the couple who own and run a company together. They may have founded a small start-up and nurtured it to grow, as in our case story *Food for Fridays*. The couple as business owners and developers is discussed, for example, in *Couple dynamics. Psychoanalytical perspectives in work with the individual, the couple and the group* (Novakovic, 2016). Another category is the romantic couple that is formed within the organization: two co-workers who get to know each other in a work context, form a couple in their personal life and possibly go on to work together. In many organizations, the presence of romantic couples is seen as a cause for concern, something to be regulated through special rules or policies. Rules and policies that do not allow couples to work together in the same workplace, explicitly encourage one of the two to find a different job or underscore the need for the couple to tone down their relationship in the workplace. This type of couple seems to activate phantasies and notions that make it necessary to regulate the couple's behaviour in order to prevent them from undermining or destroying important processes.

While the dynamics surrounding the presence of romantic couples in the workplace have been studied and described in the literature, non-romantic pairs, which are either structurally defined or based on friendship relations, have received remarkably little attention, at least in psychodynamic organizational psychology and systems theory (French, 2007) – despite the widespread presence of pairs and couples, in a broad sense, in organizational life. Pairs are a common phenomenon, and they play a vital role in the libidinal life of organizations. It is these non-romantic pairs that we set out to study in the present context.

Formal and informal pairs

Organizations contain pairs that have come together for organizational or professional reasons. Examples of professional pairs include the head consultant and the head nurse or the vicar and the organist. Sometimes, the two persons are equals in the organizational hierarchy. They are expected to work as equals on the (managerial) task and with an equal focus on the demands of the main task in their organizational unit/department or church in these examples. Some role-based pairs are subject to a clear formal hierarchy, such as director and deputy director; headmistress and head of department; CEO and secretary. In these role-based pairs, the headmistress is supposed to take the lead; the director is the deputy director's superior; and the secretary assists the CEO in their work. Another role-based pair is the line manager and the HR partner who collaborate on a task in a division of labour that is not always straightforward. Often, the roles are defined in such a way that the HR partner supports the line manager's executive work and handles tasks related to dismissals, recruitment, team development and conflict resolution. The line managers rely on the HR partner's competences but at no time gives up the executive responsibility.

All these are *formal pairs*; as such, they are defined by the organization and its main task. The pairs operate on the basis of an institutionalized division of tasks, occupying different, often complementary roles. The formal pair share an everyday life, cooperating and acting as a pair in their professional capacity. The actual pair may, but do not necessarily, develop a reciprocal loving working relationship based on their shared history, shared tasks, past or future challenges and a mutual respect for each other's contributions, including, not least, their individual experience of the other's respect for individual contributions to their shared work performance. This may, for example, include their joint handling of a difficult or critical period in the organization's life, a lengthy working relationship that gradually leads to the development of trust and respect or the collaboration on certain tasks that they develop a shared mastery of. The formal pair is viewed as a pair, and the organization inevitably also attributes them certain 'couple qualities' via projective processes and interpretations of the pair's factual as well as imagined acts. The formal pair becomes a perceived pair, a pair that others see and a pair that everyone in the organization has a perception of – the pair in-the-mind.

Workplace relations lead to the emergence of workplace pairs, some of which will be short-lived, while others are stable and long-lived constellations. A working pair could be two people who discover that they make an effective team, prefer each other as co-workers, seek each other out, often take breaks together and enjoy both their collaboration and the friendly relationship. We would say that it is love that fuels this kind of relationship. A radio host, for example, who looks forward to a shift with a certain co-worker because it is simply a little more fun, more energizing, more inspiring to do the show with that person; not that there is anything wrong with the others, but simply because this particular relationship is characterized by a certain resonance, contact, familiarity – love. Two consultants who enjoy a special feeling of trust and security in their collaboration feel well positioned to handle a complicated consultancy in an organization that is in dire need of organizational first aid. These we call informal pairs. Like the formal pair, the informal pair may be attributed certain qualities and expectations by others and have a particular role in-the-mind. They see themselves as special, and they may be perceived by others as being special. Or they may be overlooked and denied.

Both the formal and the informal pair have an attractiveness in relation to projective processes. The formal pair cannot (easily) be dismantled, and hence it may be perceived as being less susceptible to the experience and impact of projections. The informal pair is not similarly protected by the formal structure but may be a more resilient pair in their own and others' eyes, because they have actually chosen one another.

The psychology of friendship and collusion as relational dynamics

In an effort to achieve a psychological understanding of 'the pair in the organization' we will now examine the psychology of friendship and the psychodynamic concept of collusion. The concept of collusion makes it possible to understand specific divisions of labour in the form of projections and projective identifications between two individuals. Conceptually, friendship is not particularly well defined, but we attempt to develop the concept to approach a better understanding of libidinal and non-romantic workplace relations.

Friendship

Above, we mentioned the friendship pair as a type of pair found in organizations. Friendship is not a common topic in the psychodynamic literature. French, Gosling and Case (2009) address the issue of friendship as a concept and of friendship in organizations in two articles (French, 2007; French et al., 2009). We are going to take a closer look at the key points from these articles. In the articles the authors argue that friendship appears to be a rare topic in the literature on organizational psychology (French, 2007). That is paradoxical in a sense. It is a common experience that working life fosters many important relationships, including many friendships.

We view friendship as the concept best suited to capturing and describing the psychological processes at play in the workplace pair. We see the friendship pair as the 'non-romantic couple.' Friends invest libido, tenderness and acceptance of ambivalence in the relationship. They share a history as well as notions of a shared future, short or long in duration. Friends have something in common; first of all, a shared interest in the relationship but also a shared field of interest, whether it is operating a train service, party politics, the dislike of certain food products or dreams of a future utopia. Friends have loving feelings for one another, and a certain reciprocity is necessary. The relationship is not a friendship if only one of the two regards it as such. In contrast, unrequited love is not an uncommon occurrence. It is possible to love one's work tasks, organization or country, even if they do not necessarily reciprocate. Friendships are relational and fairly reciprocal. The parties may have matching or very unequal levels of libidinal investment in one another and in the relationship, a disparity that may only become apparent when one person leaves the workplace, and only one of them is interested in keeping up the seemingly close friendship.

The *Stanford Encyclopedia of Philosophy* defines friendship as follows: 'Friendship, as understood here, is a distinctively personal relationship that is grounded in a concern on the part of each friend for the welfare of the other, for the other's sake, and that involves some degree of intimacy' (https://plato.stanford.edu/entries/friendship/). In his book on friendship, the Danish PhD of philosophy and intellectual history Holst writes that friendship is based on 'the special trust and respect and loving understanding and interest in one another that characterizes their [the friends'] relationship' (Holst, 2015, p. 19). Both these definitions underscore the intimate and personal qualities that define a friendship.

As outlined above, the modern understanding of friendship defines it as emotional, private and relational. In his article on friendship and the organization, French writes that 'in the modern ideal, friendships tend ... to be seen as personal, private, voluntary, unspecialized, informal and non-contractual' (French, 2007, p. 259). While friendship was once a phenomenon that belonged to the public sphere, friendship in modern and postmodern life has been repositioned to the private sphere. Today, friendship belongs in the private domain and is characterized by intimacy, familiarity, confidentiality and acceptance, as suggested by the introductory definitions.

Like other concepts, the concept of friendship cannot be meaningfully defined independent of history and context. In the Western tradition, two different definitions from two historical periods can be identified: a modern tradition and a classic definition with roots in Greek philosophy, especially the work of Aristotle (French, 2007; French et al., 2009). In his *Nichomecean Ethics*, Aristotle he argues that friendship is not primarily a relational concept but rather a 'state of mind,' a *hexis* (French, 2007). *Hexis* is a disposition, a readiness or a capacity to act in a certain way. It is not innate but passed on or shaped through socialization. French explains, 'feelings play an important role, but the relationship is clearly not primarily personal or interpersonal, but rather indicates a set of public and political attitudes and commitments' (French, 2007, p. 259). According to French, the conceptual understanding of friendship appears to have shifted from the public to the private sphere. Today, it may seem suspect (in Western cultures) to enter into business deals with friends, but earlier in history it would be unthinkable and suspect *not* to do so or to engage in business arrangements with someone who was not a friend (French et al., 2009). Today, at least at first glance, friendship is a private matter, and mixing friendship and business may be viewed as nepotism or as unprofessional conduct.

Discussions about friendship and the historical development of the concept include such themes as deep and lasting versus superficial and fleeting relations. This issue comes up, for example, in discussions about how the social media might affect the way we relate to others. For example, it is debated whether Facebook 'friends' can be regarded as friends in a traditional sense, as we defined it above. It may appear that the broad concept of friendship that is applied in a social-media context is also finding its way into the more public domain. It is found, for example, in Holst's above-mentioned book about friendship from 2015 (Holst, 2015, p. 9). It is debatable whether virtual friendships are shallow or may, for example, have as their primary purpose to serve as a mirror to the external world, fulfilling an instrumental role in the pursuit of something other than the friendship itself. However, we also see electronic communication as a way of preserving friendship relations that are challenged by distance in time and geography. In the latter case, social media become a way to keep the friendship alive, rather than a means of self-fashioning or showcasing a particular image.

Based on studies of differences and similarities between a classic and a modern understanding of friendship, French proposes that regarding friendship not only as a relationship but also as a 'state of mind,' *hexis*, can provide a deeper understanding of friendship as the social glue in contemporary organizations and, perhaps also, as an organizing principle (French, 2007). In this view, friendship is viewed as a fundamental organizational 'structural' element, as the bureaucratic structure stops being sufficient or is gradually dismantled. This point aligns well with descriptions of contemporary organizations as being more network-based and relational in nature, less hierarchical, with greater emphasis on the personal management of one's role, which are widespread in the literature, as exemplified by Hirschhorn (2003). To propose friendship as a central organizing principle is another way to describe the libidinal nature of our working life. We view friendship as a candidate for a libidinal core in an organization. The defining qualities of friendship that were mentioned above – trust, respect, confidentiality, acceptance, loving understanding for and reciprocal interest in one another, intimacy, in-depth knowledge of one another – are not reserved for friendships in the private sphere. We see the same qualities emerging in pairs in working life, and we see that many find it desirable and attractive to develop a working-life relationship into a friendship.

The psychology of friendship

As outlined above, we regard the friendship pair as a love relationship. French does not offer many explanations of the psychology of friendship. We can demonstrate that projections, projective identification and perceptive identification are part of the dynamics of any relationship, including friendship. As such, the psychological processes we have described apply to all close relationships, including the psychology of friendship.

Friendship differs from the romantic love relationship in that it is possible to have several friendships, which may be equally profound and significant. Parents can have more than one child, and here, the difference from friendship is of a more qualitative nature – each parent–child relationship is unique and irreplaceable. Friendships too can be unique, valuable and meaningful, and we may have one best and closest friend, but the relationship is not unique and irreplaceable in the same way as family relations are. Like a marriage or other long-term romantic relationship, sibling relations or parent–child relations, a friendship may activate a wide range of profound emotions, including recognition, attachment, gratitude, understanding, envy, competition, rejection, betrayal, loneliness … But friendship covers a different span. Even if the friendship activates the same deep emotions, reaching back to one's earliest life and first relational experiences, it may offer better possibilities for perceptive identification. A friendship does not have to meet the individual's needs as fully and completely as other forms of love relationships are often expected to. We may have one friend who shares our passion for opera and another friend we go winter swimming in the icy sea. Or one friend we have deep conversations with about potentially embarrassing issues, and another friend we sing cabaret songs with. Often completely without problems. Nettleton's explanation of Bollas's concept of perceptive identification also makes an important point about friendship:

> [I]n the stage of perceptive identification it is the specificity of the object itself that is crucial. It involves the recognition that the object has an existence distinct from the self, and that the self is affected by contact with it.
>
> (Nettleton, 2017, p. 48)

This is quite compatible with Holst's reflections on the necessary degree of difference in a friendship. Friends each see themselves in the relationship as well as the other in their own right. That may be slightly easier to do in a friendship than in other love relations.

Collusion

Our past experiences from the life we have lived are present in our relationships and actions, our thoughts and emotions, conscious as well as unconscious. They may take the form of values and preferences, they shape our choices and decisions, and they affect our behaviour in relationships, including both close, personal relationships and relationships of a more professional character.

Regardless of our upbringing and the quality of our upbringing we all carry inner conflicts with us. Experiences become personality structures. Relationships and experiences with others become internal objects. External experiences may include conflict and loss, but for most of us, thankfully, they also include love, trust and nurture.

A crucial experience is the primary caregivers' capacity to contain the child's destructive and aggressive impulses, which we, like Klein and others, regard as natural aspects of the child's emotions. The capacity of the primary caregivers to contain and mirror the child's destructive and aggressive impulses is a crucial condition for the child's ability to learn to contain and express all their contradictory emotions. Regardless how careful the parental couple has been, any child will grow up with inner conflicts; they are part of the human condition. For example, it is an unavoidable and necessary experience for the child that the parents have a relationship that the child is not a part of. The child typically reacts to the parents' intimacy (conversations, kisses, comments with implicit meanings) by trying to hinder or disturb the relationship, for example by throwing a tantrum, making 'mischief' and so forth. The child is frustrated and furious over not being the centre of attention. This experience is about far more than rejection and loneliness. If the child does not experience the parents as a couple, they do not learn to stand on the outside looking in. Standing on the outside looking in, in a spectator position, provides an opportunity for having the specific experience of standing on the outside looking in at something one is emotionally attached to. That experience supports the development of the ability to think, analyse and reflect. On a fundamental level, no parents will always be able to handle the child's immediate impulses and needs. They will inevitably fail from time to time, in certain situations, and the child will internalize these experiences. However, apart from helping the child develop into a thinking and tolerable person, it is also a momentous insight for the child. There is something that I am excluded from, the world does not always work out the way I would like it to – and I can survive that.

The exact nature of the experience and its impact on a given person's development are highly individual and depend on the parents the child happens to have, the family's general life situation and context, siblings, family background and the child's personality. The experience translates into the unique version of inner conflicts the child carries with them into their future life. These inner conflicts may combine to form one or more basic themes that have a far-reaching impact, also on later adult relationships. This basic theme forms the underlying dynamic in what we describe as the collusive pair. Before we take a closer look at the psychological concept of collusion, let us look at an example:

Beth is always in doubt and finds it difficult to make up her mind. Somehow, she must have learned that trusting one's own impulses or input is unsafe or dangerous. Keith has learned that his softer sides are fairly impossible to deal with. Typically, they do not do him any good; they just bring up sad and difficult feelings that do not go anywhere. Beth and Keith have an excellent working relationship. They trust each other and know that they can rely on each other. Beth has unconsciously delegated her confidence and quick decision making to Keith, while Keith has unconsciously delegated his contact with and understanding of the more vexing emotions to Beth. Beth leans on Keith's decisions and decisiveness, and Keith has learned to appreciate the insight and understanding that Beth is able to mobilize in her work and share with him in their conversations. Beth and Keith do not include others in their close collaboration. When they work with others, they are neutral and conduct themselves properly, but it is clear that the dynamic that exists in their interactions is not present in their collaboration with other co-workers.

In the psychodynamic tradition, collusion is a concept that describes an unconscious interaction involving two or more persons, whose basic psychological conflicts fit together hand in glove and cause them to take on polarized roles in their mutual interactions. As a defence mechanism, collusion is a way of managing inner conflicts in interpersonal interactions by delegating aspects of one's basic conflict to the other. Collusion is a concept that was developed during the 1960s. It was introduced in Danish in the late 1980s by Jakobsen and Visholm (1987) in their book on couples. Jakobsen and Visholm's book refers especially to the Swiss psychoanalyst and couple's therapist Jürg Willi's writings on the concept. A collusive interaction is not necessarily conflicted. Being in love is a classic example that the object of one's love is attributed qualities and outstanding features that may have more to do with the enamoured person's phantasy than with real life. While it lasts, such an interaction may be very harmonious and happy. However, like all defence mechanisms, it comes at a cost. Let us examine Beth and Keith's interaction from that perspective.

Beth and Keith both manage an inner conflict by delegating it to the other and thus develop a collaboration that can be described as collusive in a psychological sense. That is not exclusively problematic. Their work performance is actually good and stable. However, such a working relationship has its drawbacks. They cut themselves off from working in a similarly qualitative way with other co-workers, they fail to expand their field of experience, their partnership becomes exclusive, and over time they may even risk being excluded from the wider community at work. Even though the delegation helps them both thrive in their work tasks, the pair may come to form a rigid, inflexible element in the larger group or team. Depending on the degree of rigidity in their dynamic, it may also exact an individual cost from each of them. Beth is going to continue to struggle with decision making, and indeed, the success of their partnership depends on her continued lack of mastery in this area. Similarly, Keith has to remain decisive, insensitive and lacking in empathy and thus fail to develop his empathic capacity, as long as he continues to delegate this aspect to Beth. Both are thus paying a price for maintaining this functional division of labour. Their mutual relationship may ossify, and they risk becoming clichés in the way they relate to others.

Let us delve a little more deeply into understanding this process. While collusion is a concept that describes unconscious interactions between the two persons who make up a pair or a couple, delegation is a processual concept describing the exchange of psychological material. Delegation as a psychological concept was introduced into family therapy by the German family therapist Helm Stierlin. He uses the term to describe a process where a family unconsciously charges a family member, for example a child, with completing a task on behalf of the family. An example would be the young law student who lives out their parents' dreams of an academic career or an important position in society (Bonnerup & Hasselager, 2011; Jakobsen & Visholm, 1987). Delegation is thus an unconscious psychological process where psychological material is handed to someone else (unconsciously) as a task to be completed. This delegation takes place via projective processes. In a previous publication (Bonnerup & Hasselager, 2011), we have proposed delegation as a concept that can be used to describe learning processes in groups and to understand how some members of a group are, consciously as well as unconsciously, charged with learning things on behalf of the group. This carries a high risk of becoming a 'mission impossible' and helps to explain why groups fail to learn what they think they need to learn, or why it can be so difficult to integrate experiences or competences that the group members have acquired (ibid.).

The concept of collusion helps us understand how the partners who make up a pair or a couple manifest mutual and important projective identifications for one another, coming together around a shared basic conflict. Jürg Willi categorized four themes that the collusive pair/couple usually share (Jakobsen & Visholm, 1987):

Nurture: One partner nurtures, while the other is being nurtured. In working life, we see this constellation in the relationship between the vulnerable employee who is struggling with a personal crisis and the co-worker who invests time and energy in comforting and solving the other's problems. That may be one explanation why struggling employees can receive so much support from a single co-worker, who finds him/herself completely unable to draw the line. Stepping down feels impossible, almost like a violation, even if a rational assessment might be that it is the right thing to do.

Exclusivity: Belonging together is a theme. The pair/couple closes in on itself and keeps outsiders from intruding on their relationship. For example, the pair reacts strongly to restructuring plans that split them up, placing them in separate teams/office sections. They have intense reactions if one party is seen as being 'unfaithful' by choosing to work with others or enjoying a collaboration imposed by management. They control each other and exclude the external world.

Sex: Being one's sex. A seemingly very explicit manifestation of gender roles may reflect a basic insecurity about one's own (sexual) identity. In a sense, the person overacts. The masculine or feminine expression is over the top. Sexuality is used to underpin the expression of sexual identity, and attraction is based on appearance, with the other person in a complementary role. This throws up stereotypes, such as the female secretary in stiletto heels and the male CEO in an expensive suit, which may in some cases be a manifestation of a collusive interaction.

Affirmation: The pair is drawn together by mutual affirmation. One person is cast as big, strong, decisive and admired, while the other is gentle, admiring, supportive and happy to play second fiddle. This mutual affirmation of each other's qualities keeps any insecurities or ambivalence at bay. If one person dares to criticize the other or defend a contradictory opinion, retaliation may be swift and hard.

When we propose the concept of collusion as an aid to understanding the psychological aspects of some pairs in working life, it is important to note the differences between romantic couples and their conflicts and working-life pairs and their conflicts. For pairs in working life, conflicts often take on a different scope or level, even though workplace conflicts may sometimes be quite intense and seemingly intractable. Incorporating the concept of collusion into our understanding of pairs in working life can help shed light on how the collusive aspect of some working-life pairs may dominate and thus hamper a creative work performance and the development of competences or introduce an element of rigidity into a pair or team.

Working life is full of pairs, formal as well as informal. We have attempted to achieve a psychological understanding of pairs in working life as non-romantic love relations, and we have argued that the pair is a basic psychological figure, also in working life, and that the psychology of friendship and the concept of collusion can help shed light on some of the psychological dynamics at play.

Pairs in working life

We believe that pairs in working life, in all their diversity, are love relations, in the broad meaning of love we apply in the present context. We continue with a more specific description of the types of pairs that exist and are recognized in working life. We will be presenting several illustrative cases, but first of all, we will be viewing the pairs through a different lens: what is the object of the pair's libido? We identify three different directions that the pair's libido may take. In reality, each specific pair will have a dominant manifested form, but the other forms will be simultaneously present, to varying degrees. As with any other form of categorization, this description naturally represents a simplification of all the possible variations, intricacies and combinations that exist. The three directions we see for the libido of pairs are:

1   *The libido is invested in the task.* The couple is brought together by a shared task. The main object of the libido is the task, not the relationship

itself. Over time, the pair may develop tender feelings for one another that are resistant to ambivalence. However, the primary focus is a shared experience of each other as a pair engaged in handling a shared task. A task that they both perceive as important and relevant. This springs from the bureaucratic structure, where everyone knows their role and task. That is the foundation for the pair and for their need to engage in the relationship and the shared effort to complete the task. We refer to this workplace relationship as a *marriage of convenience*.

2   *The libido is invested in the relationship.* The basic foundation for the pair is a mutual loving relationship. This relationship forms the basis for a close, libidinal collaboration. That may be a conscious choice, or it may be a meeting between the two persons' unconscious minds in a way where it is not immediately possible to determine the source of the libido in the relationship. That is what is often referred to as 'chemistry.' We call it *the friendship pair*. Another basic form is more collusive. In this case, pair is 'in love,' brought together by mutual attraction, which we regard as collusive. The two exclude others, keeping the special relationship to themselves. They may also be brought together by a desire to distinguish themselves from the rest of the organization, either through explicit criticism or through experiences that they cannot or will not express. The pair is not in contact with the others in the workplace in the same manner and on the same terms as apply to their co-workers' relationships. We refer to this as *the exclusive pair*.

3   *The libido is invested in their joint creative output.* The couple is brought together by a libidinal attachment to the work process itself and the dreams of the product of this effort. This is the creative pair, who are bound together in and by a creative process, where the energy and focus are derived from their joint accomplishment, invention, thinking or creative output. We refer to this as *the creative pair*.

4   Finally, there is a type that is not so much a pair in its own right but is instead the pair in the group and the pair that others see: *the pair as group dynamic*.

All these types of pairs occur in organizational contexts. Often as part of a group and almost always as part of an organization. The psychology of the pair is not detached from the context the pairs is a part of, and the formation of the pair affects the group and the organization they are a part of, also as pertains to the first three types of pairs. In other words, the pair is a special basic figure – a specific basic figure – in the organization. The formal formation of a pair involves an actual pair, and the development of their relationship affects the way they handle their formal tasks and roles as well as the way others perceive and respond to the pair. The informal pair is formed in a given context, the relationship contains aspects of group dynamics, and the organization reacts to the pair. Perhaps with envy and rejection, perhaps with idealization and admiration. Or with malice if the pair fails in its endeavours. In the following, we look at the four types of pairs and illustrate the dynamics by incorporating brief cases and case vignettes.

The libido is invested in the task

This pertains to the pair that has been formed with the purpose of handling a task. This marriage of convenience generally defines a formal pair, which has been formed with the purpose of completing a certain task and needs to find a way to have an effective collaboration. The object of the libido is the task at hand rather than, primarily, the relationship itself. The marriage of convenience is exemplified by Ted and Arnie, whom we meet in the following vignette.

Ted and Arnie

Ted is the newly appointed CEO of Kompus, a company that develops and manufactures compasses, mainly for pleasure crafts. For a number of years, the company has had a comfortable bottom line, but declining interest in recreational sailing now poses an existential threat to the company. Ted is charged with bringing the company through this crisis, that is what he is hired to do, and he is well aware of the responsibility. He has a good network in the industry, a nose for business and in-depth knowledge of the product line. He has previously headed at-risk organizations, and by a combination of skill and luck, he has usually managed to turn things around or at least minimize the damage – to himself and others. Arnie is the CFO and has been with Kompus for many years. He is also highly competent, has steered the endangered company through rough waters, avoiding the threat of bankruptcy. Throughout the crisis, he has sought to convince the owners of the company of the need to make cutbacks, both in the staff and in the overall budgets and the pay-outs to board members and owners.

Ted and Arnie wind up heading the company for a couple of years. Initially, Ted views Arnie as a dull bean counter, obsessed with figures and spreadsheets and without any visions, even though he is really capable within his field and area of responsibility. Arnie is sceptical of Ted's appointment. Maybe he would have liked to be the new CEO himself, after many years' loyal and dedicated work. Ted comes out of left field, driving up in a fancy car with an oversized ego. But gradually, their relationship evolves. As it turns out, Ted has some excellent ideas for new maritime products and for integrating the compass technology into other products besides maritime compasses. Arnie's skill set is crucial, as they have to raise capital for new ventures and in order to reassure the owners who are, justifiably, worried about losing the family-owned company, local jobs and, not least, a sizeable investment. Arnie keeps Ted's impulsivity in check, and Ted makes sure that Arnie does not lose heart. At one point during this development process it becomes necessary to reduce the number of employees involved in the innovation processes. Everyone expects to see the latest new hires and the unskilled labourers go first. However, Ted and Arnie put their heads together and discover that the company can let two engineers go, although it means the remaining engineers will have to take on a bigger workload, and that a couple of the young technicians can be reassigned within the company; with this, they manage to reduce the payroll without dismantling the innovation department they depend on to survive. Arnie stays loyal to the organization, and Ted becomes an accepted and well-liked CEO. The company develops, and local unskilled jobs are preserved.

The two men began their working relationship from a neutral or maybe even a negative position. Ted had no personal experience with Arnie, he respected accounting and budgets but was not passionate about it and initially perceived Arnie as a slightly pedantic bean counter. Arnie had been passed over for a position he probably had his eye on and had to accept that Ted, who might seem as a bit of a show-off, was going be in charge of the business – and Arnie's superior. Over time, they came to appreciate each other's personalities and managed to seek each other's advice and input, even when they were both aware that it might be both uncomfortable and crucially important. They both realized that with their differences each of them represented qualities that were needed to bring the company safely through. They never became friends. Arnie was reserved, he had no interest in large get-togethers and no inclination to get to know his co-workers' families. Ted was far more extrovert, and as their relationship evolved it took him a little time to realize that his and Arnie's relationship was strictly about work. Ted had young children in his current, second marriage and two children from a previous marriage, so his calendar was packed. But in the workplace context, the two men came to trust and rely on each other.

Ted and Arnie are not tied together by major creative manifestations and innovations. Nor, in any way, by an ecstatic enjoyment of each other's company or a profound feeling of meaning or appreciation. Their relationship gradually and steadily develops into a secure and trusting one. They complement each other and have each other's back. It, too, is a love relationship, although a less flamboyant one than the one playing out in our Italian import company Food for Fridays. In Ted and Arnie's relationship, determination, necessity and patience are in the foreground as the key factors defining their relationship. A love relationship that is crucially important to each of them and to the survival of the company. This workplace marriage of convenience is not a relationship based on psychological defences; it springs from the two partners' respective abilities to face the facts, embrace their own limitations and deal with their disappointments and setbacks along the way. Tolerate the ambivalence and the disagreement. It was a decision for both of them. A decision that together, they would make a good executive pair for Kompus and for one another.

It was lucky for Ted and Arnie that each of them managed to see the other's resources. In many cases, an apparent 'odd couple' never really manages to evolve. That can occur if one or both parties are limited by their own self-concept and self-perception, and where it is too demanding to relate to and trust someone who is different. Perhaps the concept of a marriage of convenience applies to workplace pairs that tend to be overlooked or do not quite receive their share of recognition.

Using the concepts of projective and perceptive identification that we introduced earlier in this chapter, we would say that Ted and Arnie manage to reduce the projective aspect quite a bit and are able to base their partnership on what is possible. Rather than a high degree of projection or identification, they see and acknowledge each other's competences and keep any potential dream scenarios in check. Thus, they do not form a creative pair but a very reality-focused pair. Their working relationship may go fairly unnoticed but is quite effective. It may also have an element of tenderness (cf. Kernberg, 1995), in the sense that each of them sees the other's personality and the difficulties they encounter along the way, without seeking to change each other. Ted sees the bean counter – but also the stable, introvert partner. Arnie might shake his head at the idea of starting a new family at Ted's age, but he also acknowledges that Ted has an appetite for life – and for women. That may sound simple, but it is no small task to manage to deal with the reality of what a partnership has to offer. It can be a tempting defence mechanism to want something different and more from the future, from the partnership or from the other's personal development than what is realistic. Instead of projecting, they each embrace their own undesired qualities, emotions and urges as they are: their own. So much easier to pass the buck and make others incorporate and play them out. Thus, even if the marriage of convenience may at first glance seem anaemic and dull, it is a love relationship that demands a high degree of maturity and ability to tolerate ambivalence from each of the partners. Thus, it has the potential to deliver a relevant and reality-oriented work performance but also to promote a personal development process or consolidation that anchors each partner more firmly in who he is. That is very different from the collusive pair.

The libido is invested in the relationship

When the main object of the workplace pair's libido is the relationship itself, we see friendship as the dominant psychological figure – and, in some cases, the collusive relationship. The former we call the friendship pair, which we regard as an important pair in organizational contexts. Here, the partners connect in a loving relationship. In some cases, an actual and real friendship gradually emerges. From the outset, the friendship pair has a strong perceived mutual sympathy and understanding. The friendship pair is not necessarily a relationship that develops into friendship, but the partners have a libidinal investment in each other that emerges from mutual affinity. They enjoy working together, and the loving feelings are an important part of the fabric supporting their joint work performance. This stands in contrast to the previous pair, which was formed entirely around the work performance. The friendship pair may have or develop a high degree of trust and intimacy and share important parts of their lives with each other, but that is not essential. What is essential is the sense of trust and intuitive sense of sharing important experiences and values. One of the 'famous' pairs in Danish political history was Lilli Gyldenkilde from the Socialist People's Party and Kirsten Jacobsen from the Progress Party. They appeared as friends who genuinely liked each other, despite stark differences in convictions and political points of view. They may have shared certain basic values, but disagreed about how to realize them. The libido in their relationship must have been founded in a friendship, not in a shared work performance.

In our main case, Food for Fridays, Fabio and Ethan become friends, but the friendship is challenged as years go by. Where our story left them, they probably do not view each other as friends. But they are also not indifferent to each other. With Holst's (2015) understanding that there has to be a certain distance between friends, that there has to be something to explore and something to keep to oneself, so to speak, Fabio and Ethan are bound by a mutual affinity for one each other, an interest in developing and creating as well as a difference of opinion about how important hard work is for achieving one's goals. Their differences may spring from each partner's personal history, emerging work experience and individual core. In each their way, they may see Food for Fridays as an adult playground. Ethan and Fabio may also be bound by the development of an actual creative product. In that case, the libido in their relationship would be invested more in what they can create together. As evident from their history at Food for Fridays, there are probably elements of both at play.

In the friendship pair and in the marriage of convenience, the parties are not blind to each other's weaknesses, inadequacies and annoying idiosyncrasies. It is not a matter of showing each other gentle tenderness. Annoying sides *are* annoying, idiosyncrasies are bothersome, and it can be really frustrating when one partner wants to finish a task, and the other insists of performing an umpteenth – or merely a second – quality check. That is demanding and cumbersome. It is a drag. However, a mutual affinity or the determination to complete a joint meaningful task can help to stabilize the relationship beyond the individual incidents that may be experienced as parts of the relationship but which do not define it in full. The opposite of love, as discussed earlier, is indifference.

The collusive pair resembles a friendship pair, but it is not the same. At the risk of oversimplifying, a characteristic of the collusive pair is that projective identification processes play a bigger role, at the cost of perceptive identification, and we maintain that different variants of both projective and perceptive processes are a part of any relationship. An illustrative case vignette:

Anna and Sasha are friends. They enjoy each other's company and like to chat during breaks. It is not that they do not dare to have differences of opinion; they simply do not. 'Anna and me ...,' says Sasha, 'Sasha and I ...,' says Anna. They text each other after work, going over the day's events. If something important happens in a staff meeting, they look at each other and each one knows what the other is thinking. The other co-workers are okay, but working with them just is not the same. Anna and Sasha almost seem to be in love, still, after four years. They prefer not to work with others. Why go through the trouble, since they do so well if only they are allowed to work the way they like? Doing a shift with someone else in their team is not nearly the same, and they often try to swop shifts, so they wind up working together. Anna and Sasha exclude the other co-workers. Their relationship is based on a collusion that confirms the internal dynamic, 'you're knowledgeable, I'm smart,' 'you're decisive, I'm reflective,' based on a number of basic themes, as described in the conceptual discussion of collusion. This is not friendship, it is closer to being in love, where the partners mutually affirm and support each other. It is difficult for most people to balance decisiveness with reflection, and it might seem easier to split up the positions.

One of the problems with collusion is the potential for fatigue. It may begin to feel too one-sided to be 'the decisive one' if one is truly in doubt. It can be difficult to be 'the smart one' if one feels stupid. The partners' respective personalities are insufficiently developed. The collusive relationship is also a defence against coming into contact with reality. What if both partners are stupid, not smart? What if decisiveness is of little use in the given situation? Sasha and Anna's relationship may spark envy, the co-workers might think, 'we too want to be part of this wonderful, passionate relationship!' They may feel excluded from an exciting relationship. Working life also contains routine tasks and requires the ability to engage in these routine tasks and realize their potentials. The 'infatuated' pair's passion may thus increase the others' sense of being stuck in humdrum routine. Infatuation gives us the sense of being special! Unique. A close love relationship between to co-workers excludes the other team members. Sasha and Anna's relationship acknowledges and showcases that some people are more interesting to some people than others. They might also become jealous of each other's other contacts. Thou shalt have no other friends before me!

The collusive pair can be an inspiration to others. They may develop into a creative pair or a friendship pair, provided they give up their infatuation or push it into the background and orient toward reality – provided the relationship allows for them to see other people. That takes maturity and requires that the collusive processes are reduced in intensity, a reality-corrected contact with the world and the ability to tolerate the fear of the potential threat from other relationships.

The libido is directed at what the pair create together

Sometimes co-workers get together and develop a particularly creative relationship. Together, they can create something that did not exist before, and which is purely a product of their collaboration, as what they find they can do together goes far beyond the mere sum of their separate accomplishments. They come to function as a particularly creative pair. We shall look at a vignette of such a creative pair.

Luke and Mia are both development consultants in a large organization. Luke has been in the organization for a number of years, and Mia joined the organization a few years ago. They work in a department where some projects are handled by individual consultants, who have their own areas of expertise, while other, larger projects are handled by consultants working in pairs or small teams. Luke and Mia share the responsibility for a large and important area for the organization. They soon discovered that working together to develop strategies, action plans, sub-projects and so forth was really satisfying and fun. That they had new ideas, developed plans and achieved exceptional results, which they were both very happy with – as was their supervisor. When Luke and Mia sit down together to develop ideas, they forget time and place. They will be so absorbed in their work that hours can go by without them noticing. They debate, experiment and get frustrated, occasionally being on the verge of yelling at each other. They listen, focus on each other, connect with each other's ideas. They laugh, wonder and are sometimes surprised at what they come up with. Other co-workers might stop by and try to join the process, but usually they will not be let in. Luke and Mia are a super-creative duo, and they both feel that they are much better together than they are when they work separately. Their shared creative process is a playful process. When they play they tend to forget what they are supposed to accomplish, and for a while they do not focus on the outcome. They also know that play takes the time it takes. It takes time for them to get into the right spirit. They can set aside time for it, but they are not fully in control of the process, since they never know exactly when they will get into the creative flow.

Luke and Mia are development consultants, but they might just as well have been product developers, writers, scientific researchers or students. Or they could be teachers planning a course. They do not always play, but when they play they are aware that is what they are doing, and they make sure to leave the process as it is, without forcing it into a specific framework, concept or formalized stages. Their co-workers are both envious of them and happy for them. Sometimes others can join the play; sometimes little drops of knowledge emerge from Luke and Mia's play. Sometimes they come up with something brand-new, exceptional, exciting. Sometimes the process just results in them having a good time together, emerging happy and encouraged and with renewed inspiration for their everyday tasks.

The creative or playful pair may form a stable and durable working relationship, which may eventually develop into a relationship on a different level: a personal friendship, co-founders of a new company or accomplishments that they will think back on with satisfaction and pride. The creative pair may also be a short-lived, even fleeting constellation that exists briefly or in glimpses as part of the many working processes and working relationships that many of us are involved in. The creative pair has a special ability to make room for a co-creative process. It is a special kind of relationship, a special form of love, that emerges in a creative friendship. To explore it further, let us take a look at the concept of play from a psychoanalytic perspective.

Play as concept has been described in many contexts, involving both children and adults. In psychodynamic theory, Winnicott is one of the leading thinkers with regard to play (Winnicott, 1971). Winnicott does not consider play to be either reality or fantasy. He highlights play as a fundamental way of being for the child. Any attempts by adults to imbue play with meaning or purpose negate play. Play is inherently without a purpose. Play unfolds in what Winnicott called the potential space. The potential space is simultaneously an imagined and a perceived space. It forms between the infant and the mother and is simultaneously internal and external, phantasy and reality. Plays is seen as a key activity in the potential space. In this potential space, the child's creative and imaginative experiments are facilitated by the mother's relevant presence and acknowledgements of the child's needs. The mother is responsible for providing sufficient and appropriate room in her concrete physical nurture for the child and in her psychological support: offering adequate and predictable reactions to the child's behaviour, recognizing and mirroring the child's emotions without being overwhelmed by them herself – what is known as *holding* in Winnicott's terminology (Winnicott, 1971; Bonnerup & Hasselager, 2011). In the potential space the normal laws of nature do not apply. In principle, everything is possible at once. The experiences made in the potential space subsequently need to be connected with reality. For example, the child may play at being a fire fighter, but in case of a real fire in the home, the child should know to stand back and let the adults take over. The ability to distinguish between the potential space and reality is a key condition for a normal development (Bonnerup & Hasselager, 2011). The potential space is a potential source of both play and creativity and what Winnicott calls 'the enjoyment of the cultural heritage' (Winnicott, 1971, p. 108). The potential space is a setting for creative experiments that are simultaneously 'safe' because they have the form of experiments and 'risky' or significant because the playful and creative processes actually have the capacity to influence the reality that the individuals subsequently find themselves in. The ability of adults to create and use a potential space in their mutual interactions depends in part on the experiences they bring with them into working life and, not least, on the organization's culture and management practices.

The potential space is a place where individual learning can be translated into organizational practices. It is a place where we can explore, debate, test and juggle many different ideas all at once. It is also a place where emotions arise and are expressed, for better and worse. Play only functions as a transitional space as long as those playing realize they are playing and know that play has a finite duration – but also that play contains a paradox: play is also reality. Play is not the connection between phantasy and reality, it is simultaneously phantasy and reality. That paradox constitutes the inherent creativity of play, not a deliberate clash between wishes and reality. Games can form a link between play and reality. The game of Monopoly does not involve actual streets and companies; the rules imitate the rules that govern the real world, and most people enjoy winning much more than losing. However, such a game is not play. Play is a different sphere; for example, the limitations of reality are suspended but still exist. It is possible to travel to the moon while remaining on earth. Luke and Mia play when they develop their projects, and they invest considerable libido in playing. They have all the time in the world to explore the possibilities, at the same time as they know that play has to stop at some point, at which time they will need to translate the creative content into organizational activity with everything that the implementation of new initiatives entails. A training course, a development process, a new product all include elements of play as well as planning and an orientation toward reality, the external world, economics and documentation requirements. Translating creative processes into real change or tangible products takes hard work and a – potentially tedious – implementation process with things to do, write down, arrange, remember and plan. Those organizational activities sit alongside play as a condition for turning creativity into practice. In a sense, innovation not only requires creativity but also a considerable number of operational routine tasks.

Thus, the creative pair in working life never simply arrive at real accomplishments through play alone. Play is driven by pleasure and libido. Play can take us to new places but cannot be directed. The creative pair approach their work task through play. In play, the purpose-driven direction is suspended, but afterwards, it is of course both possible and necessary to translate the insights gained in play into purposeful behaviour and production.

The creative pair is driven by the desire for or ambition of creating something new. Engaging in an intimate psychological space requires a high degree of openness between the participants. It requires them to surrender control for a time, leaving the work-related rationale aside and allowing themselves to dream or speak freely, because they know that the dialogue may produce a good idea. The creative pair may spark envy, and it may be exclusive. The intimate working process and the exchange of ideas do not allow for others to be included in the relationship. They do not invite others to join them in play.

The pair as group dynamic

The pair as group dynamic is a pair that has formed as a group defence; this defence is disguised as love but it is not love in the sense of the word in the present book. Thus, the pair may resemble – and even be mistaken for – a romantic couple. Like other group dynamic processes, it may play out and be perceived as an individual or a relational process. It is easier to spot the manifestation of the dynamic than group dynamic as such. Elsewhere, we have referred to this as the group disguised as an individual (Bonnerup & Hasselager, 2008); in the present context, we will describe it as the group creating a pair.

In Bion's famous work on group mentality and basic-assumption mentalities he identified the third basic group assumption as 'pairing' (Bion, 1968). A pairing group acts as if its key purpose is to meet to create a pair that in turn will create a child – a Messiah. A pairing group will often be perceived as cheerful, slightly flirtatious, driven by pleasure and completely conflict-avoidant and denying reality. The members appear to be having a good time and seem to be productive, but at the cost of banishing disagreement and difficulties from the group's reality. The Bionic pair springs from the group's desire to bring about something new. The group's basic assumption is that by creating a pair, which in turn can create a Messiah, the group can achieve salvation from its present perceived, imagined or real problems. The Bionic pair is a defence, a dream, a possibility. The group wants to create a Messiah, but he should not be realized. We have a case about such a Bionic pair.

Sandra and Martin work in an HR department as HR partners. They have both been with the organization for a few years and generally enjoy their work. Last month the department was handed a big assignment, which has top management's meticulous and demanding attention. At the departmental meeting, everybody soon agreed that Sandra and Martin were qualified to take on the task. Sandra and Martin were honoured to receive this vote of confidence from their co-workers, but they were also a little concerned – maybe some of the others would have liked the project for themselves? Were the others not at all envious that Sandra and Martin were handed the task – and what about the head of the department? He had suggested that the two handle the project together, but why had he picked them in particular? However, the atmosphere was friendly, and the encouragement from the others seemed sincere. Surely, Sandra and Martin would be able to handle this strategically important task in a good way.

As Martin was on his way out the door after the meeting, it occurred to him that all they really took away from the meeting was the team's enthusiastic support. The many good ideas were actually rather vague, the experiences the others contributed were fairly generalized, and there was a complete absence of critical voices, which was quite out of character for the team. Although Martin had often wished he could be spared the more experienced team members' sage advice, he had a feeling that he had missed something. Eventually he shrugged off the feeling. Looked forward to working with Sandra, who was a talented, competent and attractive woman. For her part, Sandra was overwhelmed by an inexplicable sense of unease as she was heading home. She found herself suddenly yearning for her days as a preschool teaching assistant, when she would often forget to come in from the playground to attend the lunch-break staff meeting; that was 'for the adults,' she thought then, until she remembered that she was one of them. Sandra was aware that she was prone to worrying and tried to convince herself that she had no reason for concern. Anyway, she would be working with Martin, whom she really liked. He was a little more experienced than her, and if he was not worried, there was hardly any reason for her to have misgivings.

Sandra and Martin took on the project, conducted internal interviews and met with top management to present their preliminary plans and ideas. Management was basically quite pleased with their ideas, but they had a number of demands and criticisms that Sandra and Martin noted. As previously arranged, they presented their project, ideas, plans and the additional demands at a meeting in the HR partner team. The team's response was deafening silence. No criticism, no praise. Nothing. Sandra and Martin were confused, they looked at each other, looked at their co-workers who gazed into space, looked down, sneaking a peek at their watches or iPhones. With disbelief, Sandra and Martin heard the team leader round off their presentation by saying, 'Well, that looks all right, I'll take a closer look at it some time over the next few days. Let's move on to the next point in the agenda, shall we?' The team members stirred a little, many topped off their coffee, and the meeting continued. Martin was astonished – what was that about? Sandra thought about walking out or speaking up to say that she did not understand what was going on, but she was not sure if she could do it without breaking into tears, so she stayed silent.

The group has created a pair and charged them with delivering a Messiah. Something new. The co-workers and top management are not silent because they do not care. Their indirect message is rather, 'Do it! Create a good result! You, of all people, can do it, we can't. But be advised, we'll punish you if you fail. Oh, and by the way, the punishment will be even harder if you succeed. You need to remain a hope, not a real-life solution.'

The project was so prestigious and crucial for the department's reputation that setbacks or failure were inconceivable. The team leader fell out of role and became a team member. The fear was so overwhelming that denial of risk was the only option. Sandra and Martin went back to work with even greater dedication, and, to cut a long story short, they were largely successful. There were a few snags along the way, but they were dealt with, and management was fairly happy with the outcome. However, Sandra and Martin were left with the HR partner team's devaluation of their efforts and results. During the project and at its conclusion others shared many tips and ideas for what they could have done differently; ideas that no one had offered at the outset. The group could not quite conceal their glee over the criticisms that were raised after the project was concluded, despite a fairly good outcome. Sandra and Martin were punished for failing to realize a flawless Messiah and instead delivering merely a good enough baby. Or maybe they were punished for succeeding.

The group dynamics were so powerful that if Sandra and Martin had landed a total success, the group might well have felt compelled to destroy what they had created by devaluing it. Idealization was an attempt at avoiding rivalry and avoiding expressing envy and resentment, and when the perfect outcome failed to materialize (in part because no one had offered relevant input and critique), rivalry became a possibility, since, by then, the group had already picked the losers. Envy was transformed into concern for the carefully selected slings and arrows aimed at the pair or into poorly concealed gloating – it was inevitable, putting two young and inexperienced people in charge of such a crucial project ...

If we were to see Sandra and Martin detached from the group dynamic, they might form a creative pair or a friendship pair. They liked each other and enjoyed committing themselves to completing a complicated and demanding task that called for professional competence, innovation and creativity. That is part of the story too. However, in the case, the group dynamic that unfolds around them is the dominant factor. In that sense, Sandra and Martin are a pseudo pair, because their dynamic is primarily associated with the group; the pair is created by the group dynamic, in particular by the group's defence, not by their own libido in relation to either the task or the relationship.

The pair that others see

The working-life pairs we have described are of course simplifications. Real-life working pairs will be unique hybrids containing elements from most types, and what occupies the foreground may vary over time. In this last description of the pair as group dynamic, it is clear that a pair is also, always, the pair that others see. Even if the pair's dynamic should not primarily be understood as a group dynamic, any pair is always a pair in relation to others. Working-life pairs are seen and perceived. The pair is a basic figure, and a basic figure also gives rise to basic-figure feelings in others. Seeing pairs who have a mutual attraction, for example, can spark many different and sometimes intense emotions, including yearning, jealousy, envy and a sense of inferiority.

A given pair may well perceive their own role as that of a marriage of convenience between two equals, while their co-workers or staff perceive them as domineering mother and father figures, who mirror and are mirrored in the others' personal experiences with 'authority pairs.' The staff may not be able to attempt to see the real pair, but instead see the authority pair as they perceived – and remember perceiving – the most important authority pair from their childhood. For some, this includes experiences of betrayal and unreliability; for others, experiences of detachment and self-absorption; and for yet others, experiences of attention and nurture. The authority pair sparks a wide range of emotions. Leading and following and subjecting oneself to others' decisions are processes fraught with emotion (Gabriel, 1999). The authority pair may find that are being pigeon-holed, unable to break free. Whatever they try to do, it will always be interpreted in relation to their employees' own frame of reference. A process that is more projective than perceptive. Inherently, we all carry with us basic figures of pairs, based on our own personal history and experiences. Experiences with pairs that we were and are a part of, and which others are a part of, and, not least, the experience of being left out.

Loving relations spark more than warm feelings. Love, by its nature, cannot extend to everyone. Those who are on the outside, either working with or observing the working pair, will have different reactions, for different reasons, to the pair. They may feel envy when they see the friendship pair's obvious pleasure at working together. The passion that unfolds within the creative pair may also trigger yearning or envy. Both the exclusion and the passion can make others feel rejected, dull, incompetent. Success can often breed envy in others, who feel less accomplished. The pairs have to be willing to face off continuous envious attacks and maintain their collaboration to the extent that it is appropriate in relation to the overall work performance. They have to consider when it is helpful to keep working as a pair, and when it is necessary or more effective to open up the dyad. Love-filled relations are important for a good working life. But they are not something we can control.

Love of the task

The workplace pairs in all their diversity are not the only love relations working life has to offer. In the following we look at another libidinal relationship: that between the employee and the work task. We take a closer look at motivation and passion and at what drives dedicated employees. We look at love of the task, at work as seduction and at motivation, meaning and necessity.

The relationship between the employee and the work task is far more than a technical relationship to be rationalized and rendered efficient. Many people invest not only time and energy but also commitment, creativity and passion in their work. To many of us, our relationship with our work and, not least, the work tasks plays a large and central role for our self-perception and our sense of accomplishing something meaningful. For many, work is not merely a necessary evil that we have to endure to pay our bills; on the contrary, it often plays a role in both defining and developing our identity to varying degrees, depending on the specific possibilities of the given job or profession. Most people have some sort of attachment to the work tasks they perform and the organization the tasks are performed in. To some, the work tasks and the professional field are the main focus, for others it is the organization, but in any case, it is our claim that almost everyone – regardless of personality, training and organizational attachment – identifies with their job and their work tasks. It makes a difference how involved we are in other identity spheres besides our work. An actuary who exclusively identifies with and develops within their profession will be more vulnerable to organizational events than a colleague who is also passionate about synchronized swimming and active in the local ramblers' club. The latter has the option of relying on other sides of their identity if, for example, something makes it difficult or impossible to remain an actuary, or when work involves frustrating setbacks.

Work is important. It is our argument that the way we relate to work tasks can be understood as a love relationship. A love relationship that may be quite passionate, mainly rational, exclusive or creative. In the mid 20th century, organizational theories began to include a general interest in the content of the work. During the previous decades, the focus had been on the importance of social relations and appreciation, but now there was a growing awareness of our need to apply our intellectual resources and our need for a job that offered continuous opportunities for learning and development. The new theories challenged the sharp distinction between mental and manual labour, which, although it had proved effective in the early 20th century, could no longer satisfy the needs of contemporary employees or organizations. Motivational and learning theories gained ground, and engagement, responsibility and continuous learning and development became key focus areas for organizational theory and practice (see, e.g., Illouz, 2007; Senge, 1990).

New motivational theories (e.g., McGregor's Theory X and Theory Y or Maslow's Hierarchy of Needs) sought to address the important question of how to motivate employees to invest their time, resources and commitment in their work and to do so over long, continuous periods. Burkard Sievers writes in the essay 'Motivation as invention' (Sievers, 1993) that motivation comes into play only as a surrogate for meaning, arguing that meaning, or the loss of meaning, constitutes the underlying issue that is addressed in concerns about motivation. In our experience, motivation is a complex issue. In some workplaces, (the lack of) meaning and the resulting (lack of) motivation are a problem. Certain work tasks and routines appear pointless to those who perform them and hence do not help to build motivation and may even undermine it. Midwives, for example, point to the hours they spend on paperwork after a delivery – time they would prefer to spend with pregnant women and women in labour – as a task that they find boring and pointless. Today, it seems easy to find examples of unnecessary but mandatory paperwork, but requirements to attend staff meetings or to pass on knowledge from training courses and so forth may also be perceived as pointless.

Paradoxically, we also encounter the opposite problem. Work that is too meaningful. Where supervisors need to remind their employees to stop working when their workday is over, to hold their own work performance up to realistic quality standards, to clock off and tend to activities and obligations that are not work-related, whether it is picking up the kids from school and spending time with them, doing sports or other recreational activities or simply kicking back and recharging their batteries on the sofa. That is often referred to as work–life balance – an interesting phrase where 'work' is seen as the polar opposite to 'life' – a balance that is also a challenge to many in executive positions. In our experience, many today find that work offers an abundance of meaning, and that engaging in work tasks, processes and relationships is seen, in a sense, to hold its own reward – to the extent that it is overdone. Too much meaning is stressful too. We see a certain degree of fatigue in people's engagement in organizations. People learn to say 'oh, well,' take their tasks less seriously, live with what is often referred to as '80% solutions' or 'good enough,' referencing Winnicott's 'good-enough mother.' People are encouraged to take changes and cutbacks 'on the chin,' but at the same time, dismissals in connection with downsizing are made with reference to the individual employee's productivity. Publish or perish. Document. Develop. Sometimes people find that they struggle to find time for their main tasks in the organization, as the paperwork eats up more and more of their time. Or they do not understand that their main tasks include documenting the completion of tasks. It is not always easy to see the point of the documentation requirements. It might seem a waste of time to document that Mrs Jones's potted plants were watered but less pointless to make a record of her medication to prevent temps and nincompoops from doing serious harm.

But what drives this passion, this libidinal relationship with the work tasks? Hirschhorn writes that in addition to having work tasks that are perceived as important, much of the psychological explanation stems from the passionate employee's (unconscious) sense of limitations and incompleteness, which is resolved in the meeting with the task (Hirschhorn, 2001). Essentially in the same way as in romantic love – when I am with the unique and amazing object of my love I can be whole. Thus, the passion for the task involves an external relationship: the task is exciting, important, meaningful. I can help deliver products, services or results that matter to others, maybe to many. I work for a good or important cause that matches my values or beliefs. There is also an internal relationship: a simultaneous sense that working with the meaningful task helps make me whole and complete. Let us look at a concrete example.

Love of the task: Vita

Vita loves her work. She always has. From she was young she has known that she wants a job where she can be involved in coming up with something new, something with a higher purpose. She trained as a biologist and joined a research unit in the pharmaceutical industry. She enjoys being part of a research team, involved in uncovering ground-breaking new knowledge and treatments for diseases that are particularly prevalent in the third world. In time, the knowledge they develop will probably be translated into cures for large groups of people. The actual commercial breakthrough is still years into the future, but for Vita, the main motivators are, first, that she is developing new knowledge and, second, that this knowledge can benefit large groups of people. Sometimes, she even admits to herself that this is the order of her priorities. She loves going to conferences and being someone who presents knowledge that others do not have. As much as she loves going to conferences and being in the spotlight, being someone with (considerable) knowledge, she also loves the quiet days in the lab and at her desk. Reading, examining, analysing, learning. Lunch with her colleagues, whom she likes and respects, the late afternoons at work, often turning into evenings, as she forgets to come home. Her family has more or less accepted that this is what she is about. Her husband also works long hours and is deeply passionate about his work – albeit not quite as passionate as Vita – so he knows what it means to be able to get stuck in. The children, who are now in middle school, know that their mother is never the one who bakes cake for school events or is active in the well-being group; for good and bad, she is the mother who often asks the teachers to set more ambitious learning goals for the children.

In addition to her job, she has joined a scientific society, which she recently agreed to chair. Whenever she can find the time she works on a paper to be submitted to an international journal. This may sound like a stressful working life, but it is not. Vita is thriving. Big time. Occasionally, she is tired. Occasionally, she would like to be able to take an entire weekend off. Occasionally, she notices that her husband and children think that she is too distant. But they know that she would not thrive in any other job, and that she would not be a good mother or a happy wife if she was less committed to her work.

For example, when she makes time for a family lunch, she often catches herself thinking that it would be more meaningful to work on her paper. On Saturday evenings, when they do family night with TV, games, sweets for the kids and wine for the parents – family nights that she know will soon be a rare occurrence, as the kids will want to go out with their friends instead – she often gets an uncontrollable urge to quickly, quickly throw a glance at a lab result; quickly, quickly check her email; quickly, quickly jot down a good idea. Sometimes she takes her phone with her to the lavatory to make a note of something, so her family will not complain that she is working again because she could not bear forgetting a good idea she had in the middle of a game of Monopoly. If she has any complaints, it would be that she does not sleep well, and that she and her husband cannot agree on holiday plans. She would like to go to Crete (where she could spend a couple of hours every day working on her paper), but her husband would rather go sailing, where there is no room or time for her to check up on her projects.

There is no doubt that Vita loves her work and her work tasks. But what is it she loves? She loves creating something new. Being the one who creates something new and being seen and recognized for creating something new. It is motivating for her to apply her competences to something that has an existence outside herself. Something that will live on after she is gone, that has a life of its own and which benefits others. It is possible (quite likely, in fact) that no one is ever going to erect a statue in memory of her magnificent contributions and that she will never be awarded a Nobel Prize for her work, but (a little) less will do. Other scholars are going to build on the knowledge she creates, and she is well-respected within her academic community. That is satisfactory in a narcissistic sense, but it is also satisfying in a concrete sense.

Something is being created. Love of the task, including love of the creative process (the professional practice), the resulting product and the recognition she receives for her work (narcissistic satisfaction). Creativity is highly motivating. She is proud of her work, just as she is proud of her children, who are about to begin to build their own lives and their own commitments.

The kind of commitment to the task that Vita displays is only possible if it also satisfies an inner need. In relation to the concept of passion that we outlined above, in this case we might say that Vita's considerable commitment and passionate working life are also driven by some sense of incompleteness inside her. Something she is resolving for herself through the way she handles her working life. Binney, Wilke and Williams (2003) have explored this topic. They conducted a large number of interviews with managers on many levels and summarized their analysis in the book *Leaders in transition – the dramas of ordinary heroes* (Binney, Wilke & Williams, 2003). Like Hirschhorn, they focus on the leader's psychology to explain what drives individual, at times extraordinary, performance. They argue that it is not enough to look at competences such as decisiveness, analytical skills, strategic abilities or, for that matter, any of the other skills or competences that are highlighted in the management literature. What drives the individual to want to be 'the chosen one,' to put in the persistent effort that is sometimes required? They argue that we all have a so-called 'inner worm,' an inner conflict, based on our childhood history, which constitutes a crucial inner motivation shaping our love of the task (ibid., pp. 187ff). These inner issues that have grown out of our personal history are often regarded as weaknesses or flaws. Something we need to fix, sort out, if we begin to notice it. Binney et al. point out that rather than viewing the 'inner worm' as a weakness or a flaw, we could take a more nuanced view. Our history helps make us who we are, for good and bad. These inner insecurities or demons are also what compel us, they are our source of energy. Our inner unconscious forces can contain both destructive and self-destructive elements and potentials for healing and development. Let us see what Vita's 'inner worm' might look like.

It might look as follows: Vita has a demanding super-ego. She has an inner compulsion always to be active, to be productive. She remembers her grandmother who loved reading. Bent over her book while knitting. It was inconceivable to waste time by simply reading. Her grandmother, who always finished off the leftovers from the dinner table in the kitchen to make sure nothing went to waste. Her grandmother, who always kept her flat spotless. Truly spotless. And her parents' shared admiration for her grandmother's desire to be productive. Their recognition of the effort it took to raise two children on her own and make a good life for them. Vita's parents had always worked hard, and they had few kind words about anyone who was unable to pull their weight and provide for themselves. Vita's mother's brother had never really got a grip on life; he eked out a living based on welfare and temporary jobs. Although her parents had never said anything to her uncle's face, at the dinner table at home they had often talked about how he ought to pull himself together. Somewhere inside, Vita had a fear of missing a step and being thrown off the merry-go-round of working life, unable to ever climb back on. A fear of failure and its consequences. From Vita's perspective, a performance that was less than sublime was the same as failure. As long as she was committed to her work, she was able to keep these thoughts at bay, almost like 'the unthought known' (Bollas, 1987), but in quiet moments, she felt a sense of unease and emptiness, verging on anxiety, making her nervous, prickly and irritable. In that sense, Vita might be right that the children were better off with her busy at work.

That might seem like a good and creative compromise between inner conflicts, possibilities and self-expression. As long as Vita can handle it, as long as her husband is accepting of it, and the children are thriving. But what if they do not? What if Vita falls ill? If her husband decides he has had enough? If the children develop problems that require a more focused presence in their lives? If Vita is laid off? If she retires? The immediate problem might be that Vita has so little experience with expressing herself creatively and productively in other domains besides working life. She simply has not learned any other ways of realizing her love of working and being useful. Essentially, she would find it difficult to do something simply because it is interesting or fun or enjoyable for her. The compelling voice from her super-ego instructing her to be useful and perform in order to have right to exist would no longer find a natural expression in the demands of her working life. It might become an existential problem for her to exist simply for the purpose of existing. Working and feeling profound and intense love of her work and her work tasks are parts of Vita's identity. The problem would be that her identity is so deeply intertwined with her working life. Another problem might be that she underestimates her own importance for her family; that there is a quality in sharing moments and experiences together, and that they would like to have her be more present. To have Vita discover it is actually possible to read a book *without* knitting at the same time. She might also be troubled by her perceptions of others' perceptions of her. She would probably imagine that they saw her as a sponge, a layabout, a bore; and with little connection to reality, she might perceive herself as similar to her uncle, based on her own unrealistic notions of the way others perceive her.

In her demanding and fulfilling work, Vita invests libido in her work tasks. She would have to withdraw this libido and direct it at something else. This could be the beginning of a new, exciting chapter in her life, or it could become the impetus for resolving a problem that might have emerged within the family. It might also develop into a manic preoccupation with some minor cause or transgression that she would be unable to put aside because it had become too important to her, and because it would be difficult for her to find something else that held the same potential for commitment and enthusiasm.

It might also take a less definitive form. For example, she might fail at a project. Get a new supervisor who had a less glowing assessment of her talent. A research finding from another company might challenge Vita's conclusions and knowledge or put them into a different perspective. The foundation Vita is standing on might be shaken. A 'one-sided love relationship' with the work task infers a potential vulnerability that can easily lead to an exaggerated assessment of the risk associated with changes. As a result, even minor changes may be felt as – and actually become – catastrophic. Thus, the person's love of the task can become an obsession. Vita *has to* love and continue to love her work. That becomes a problem in itself due to the imbalance and lack of freedom it produces.

If the love relationship is obsessive, meaning that the person is driven by an inner compulsion to love or be passionate about their work, resigning or retiring becomes impossible. If it is impossible to leave, the relationship loses its voluntary quality and instead becomes symbiotic. The distance that Holst describes as a necessary aspect of friendship is also necessary in our relationship with our work tasks. If it is lacking, even minor setbacks or losses may be (perceived as) catastrophic. That is a real risk for Vita. If her passionate relationship with her work is in fact an unconscious effort to fill up or complete the self, to use Hirschhorn's terminology, failure is not an option for her. That puts her at risk of accepting a high cost for staying – perhaps too high a cost. The voluntary relationship becomes a compulsion, and the necessary critical distance is lost.

Another risk is that Vita's challenges, major or minor, turn to emptiness. However, we should not forget that Vita's 'inner worm' is also what drives her commitment to a job that she profits from. She puts her time and her life to meaningful use, she receives recognition for her accomplishments, and she is engaged in activities that she finds relevant and useful.

When does the passionate love relationship with our work tasks become a problem? When is it too much, unhealthy, maladaptive? Would it be better if Vita (and all the other committed and hard-working employees with her) did not have worm holes in their selves that they sought to full up with work? The question is hypothetical. In fact, we all have experiences we wish to complement, complete, put behind us. We are not talking about using traumatic experiences as fuel, but about inner notions, incomplete experiences, repetition urges driven by the hope of new and different experiences.

Our unconscious is at work. If we accept Hirschhorn's premise that passion consists in part of hopes and notions of completing the self, few people would probably want for a lacklustre working life completely free of passion and commitment. Binney, Wilke and Williams's metaphor of our 'inner worm' is well aligned with elementary psychodynamic theory – that we bring experiences from past relations into our present relations. Experiences that have helped make us who we are. That help us understand how elements of work tasks can be crucial to one person and trivial to another. Why and how it can seem so important to be allowed to feel and express our passion for something. That may be a grand or artistic endeavour, but the many everyday chores of an everyday working life can similarly be invested with libido and be used to express creative unconscious forces and/or desires to heal inner issues. The creative artist is not alone in drawing on their personal history, so does the recycling station manager, the rehabilitation facility social worker, the corporate VP and the HR partner in a bank.

Work as escape and seduction: Jeff

Vita has a passionate relationship with her task – a love relationship. She is dedicated. However, a work task can also offer an escape from a complicated situation. The American sociologist Arlie Russel Hochschild is the author of the 1997 book *The time bind*. Based on numerous interviews in an American company she describes the emergence of a situation where working life appears attractive and offers personal development while family life appears increasingly tightly scheduled and rigid. Many young families live a life based on strict schedules, lists of routine chores divided up between the parents and weekly rosters for taking the kids to preschool, picking them up again, shopping, cooking and so forth; a level of planning that would make a Lean consultant green with envy. Working life, on the other hand, may appear as an oasis, an attractive, pleasant refuge and a place for self-realization, meeting interesting people, coming up with new, exciting ideas, learning new and interesting things and staying up to date. To a high degree, what working life and family life have to 'offer' the individual reflects their own notions and projections. Time to meet Jeff.

Jeff is an architect. He is respected and competent, although he is not quite as respected for his competence as he feels he ought to be. With years of hard work, he has built his own company up from scratch, and he finally seems to be succeeding. He has four employees and is involved in several profitable and somewhat prestigious projects. He is personally involved in all the firm's projects, monitors everything (micromanaging, according to his staff), handles contacts with clients and authorities. Both the clients and the regulatory agencies like working with Jeff; he is accommodating, open to compromise and quick to reply and make decisions. Jeff married somewhat late in life, or, in fact he is not married but lives with his partner, Ella. They have two young children together. Ella is younger than Jeff but was a little old to have children and finds it burdensome to be a mother of young children. She is a school teacher and finds that the latest school reform made her working life harder. The reform has her spending more time at the school, with less flexibility to prepare for her classes at home in the evening, which she wishes she still could and had always imagined doing when she – finally – had children. Ella is also unhappy that they are not married. She would like a proper proposal, a church wedding and a big party. Jeff thinks it is a waste of money and would prefer to put that money into consolidating the firm instead.

Their family life is strained. There are many practical chores, and once the children have been put to bed, Ella is usually asleep in front of the TV. Jeff works evenings and weekends, going through drafts, solutions, checking up on budgets and making arrangements with contractors. Sometimes he works on a dream house, a house he imagines he might one day build, perhaps for himself, perhaps for a good client, and when Ella comes into his study, complaining that he is working again, he shows her what he is working on and explains how important it is for him to spend time on this particular project. He enjoys drawing buildings, finding solutions, building homes for others. He also stays late at the office. He enjoys meeting with clients and contractors, finding solutions, fixing problems, seeing the clients' delighted faces and interest when he presents a good and unanticipated solution. He knows that the staff feel he is meddling, but he also knows that they appreciate the opportunities for professional development the work offers, and he knows that a couple of them are hoping to make partners over the next few years. He forgets time and place when he works. Last week he forgot to pick up the children from preschool; that was obviously not his finest moment ...

For Jeff there is a big difference between the self-realization, creativity and ability to be creative that he finds in his working life and the hectic, routine character of his life as a husband and the father of toddlers. At work, he gets personal growth and development, recognition and the ability to express himself. At home, he feels that he is criticized, inadequate and dull.

Work is seductive. But what is the seductive quality? At first glance, it is the pleasure of being competent and being recognized as such. Seeing his competence mirrored in others' appreciation of his work. Seeing his competences manifested as tangible buildings and homes. Having his self-perception affirmed and seeing parts of his ego ideal realized. Those are external factors: others recognize his competences and confirm the manifestation of his ego ideal. Jeff is seen the way he wants to be seen. 'In your eyes I am who I would like to be.' There is also an inner mirroring. Jeff experiences the joy of realizing an ego-ideal (more than avoiding a punitive conscience function within the super-ego). Jeff manifests elements of the creative sides of his unconscious and is – perhaps unconsciously – met by others who experience resonance and pleasure in their collaboration and the work he does.

Jeff is also affirmed by passing something on to the next generation (of architects) rather than the hard work of caring for toddlers, providing nurture by preparing lunch packs, hanging laundry, wiping up vomit and building structures out of Lego bricks only to take them apart again. At home, with his family, he is more in contact with the judging component of his super-ego – are you doing enough? – and with demands that he does not feel like living up to. Ella's demand for a romantic wedding is not exactly romantic when it is a demand and an explicit expectation. There is nothing romantic about their relationship, while his interactions with business partners, authorities and, not least, clients, offer frequent affirmation and perhaps even idealization.

For Jeff, love of the work task is also a defence against being in contact with, not only critical assessments and demands, but also the unlimited nature of children's claim for their parents' attention and love. A defence against the sense of inadequacy that any parent lives with. There is always something one could have done differently and maybe better. Perhaps, Jeff is also trying to avoid intimacy. Perhaps he has experiences of failure, loneliness, betrayal and a constant experience of not being seen and understood as who he really is in close relationships. Experiences that are not necessarily conscious, but which shape and influence his experience, expectations and choices.

Also, work at the studio is tangible. Finite and productive. It results in buildings. In his relationship with his children he can hope that what he does is good enough, that it is sufficient and okay. He will never know for sure. As Winnicott put it, the recognition that one may eventually get is to be allowed to look after the grandchildren – 'Rewards come *indirectly*. And, of course, you know you won't be thanked' (Winnicott, 1971, p. 143) In a sense, work at the studio is seductive, because it offers real gratification that family life cannot – and maybe is not supposed to – provide.

There are certain similarities between Jeff and Vita. They are both committed and passionate in relation to their work and work tasks. In our story about Jeff, we might also attempt to describe his 'inner worm,' the thing that drives him and his need to be seen and affirmed and the thing that makes it feel better and more attractive for him to be seen and affirmed by clients, contractors and project partners than by a couple of toddlers with what he perceives as insatiable demands. There are also elements of seduction in Vita's work; something that beckons and lures her into making priorities that she might regret in the long term, looking back. However, in Jeff's case, his relationship with his work is closely tied in with his relationship with his family. His relationship with his firm and clients can be best be understood in comparison with his relationship with his wife, children and family life. He escapes into his work, avoiding having to deal with the hands-on, mundane aspects of family life and marriage. He is lured away to the 'adult playground' that his fun, creative work represents and the recognition it offers.

In Hochschild's study, which she references in *The time bind*, she describes how the employees develop strategies for handling the feeling many of them have of spending too little time with their families and frequently prioritizing work over the demands of family life. Some of these strategies involve reframing the needs of family life in order to make ends meet. For example: it is healthy for children to be home alone; it teaches them to be self-reliant. Another strategy is developing what Hochschild calls 'the potential self': as soon as we find the time, any day now, we'll all go camping, go on a month-long holiday by a lovely beach, grow our own organic vegetables. The sleeping bag that is still in its packaging, the holiday catalogues, the juicer at the back of the cabinet – they are all props in this unlived dream, which mainly serves to provide assurance that we could do something else, that there is a different life just beyond the routines of everyday life (Hochschild, 1997). Throughout, she points out how work may be experienced as personally developing and engaging, whereas family life may be experienced as a long series of Taylorized procedures, as we see it in the brief outline of Jeff's life.

Motivation, meaning and necessity: Britt

It is far from all work and all work tasks that invite creative flow experiences, seduction and buckets of commitment. There is plenty of mundane work with day-to-day routines and repetition, toil and monotony. Is it possible to love a job that does not in itself invite creative innovations and self-realization? We think it is. It is possible to feel love for a task that is inherently meaningful. It is meaningful to look after senior citizens, to fix an oil burner that breaks down during a cold snap, to set a broken shin bone so the person can walk again, to teach children to read. Not necessarily heroic efforts, but necessary and meaningful work that makes society function.

Necessity is meaning. A here-and-now necessity. Customers to assist, children to be looked after, decisions to be made. Or the necessity of community. Someone has to teach others to read, pick up the garbage, distribute district heating. It may also offer professional gratification and a way to earn a living. Love of one's work can include love of unheroic work, that is, work that does not require an extraordinary effort, and whose prime source of meaning is that is part of something bigger, a structure that keeps society functioning. The gratification of being part of a collegial community. Being part of the labour force, a contributing member of society who handles a specific task. Love for the team or profession. That sort of everyday love is exemplified by Britt.

Britt is a chief physician. For the three years that she has headed her department, she finds that she thrives more and more in her leadership position, that her staff is generally thriving, and that she enjoys widespread respect, both for her professional competence and for her leadership skills. She is usually a straight talker, likes to call a spade a spade, a problem a problem, and she likes offering brief and specific praise when her staff has excelled in a difficult case or situation. Everyone from the specialists – including the ones with very narrow, specific fields – to the nurses, assistants and orderlies like Britt's leadership style, and she generally enjoys a good working relationship with the head nurse. In other words, it works, and it works well. In Britt's own assessment, her leadership style is working because she knows her subordinate leaders well in many ways and has great confidence in both their medical judgment and their ability to handle HR issues. As a result, many of her leadership decisions are fairly uncomplicated, and she enjoys widespread support for her decisions.

Britt and many of her staff members enjoy being part of this particular team precisely because it is driven by continuity rather than change. The team has its own rituals and stories about past events. That creates a sense of belonging and attachment, a team spirit that survives even when individual members are replaced. Many doctors in training enjoy their time in the department, even if they are only there for a limited time. They find it fairly easy to get into a routine that is easy to decode.

Love for the team is based on the sum rather than on the individual parts. Occasionally, Britt has to let staff members go, and sometimes, she has to deal with difficult conflicts. But she fundamentally likes the team and is keen to develop, look after, take responsibility for and spend time with the team and the individual team members.

Sometimes her colleagues say to her teasingly that she seems to regard the department as her family. That is actually not true, however. Britt makes demands, handles dismissals, corrects mistakes and generally maintains a certain detachment with regard to her family life, which is fairly undramatic and involves a husband and three children, a suburban house, a dog and an aging mother in a nursing home. Her close relations with her staff are not of a personal nature. It pertains to the performance of the tasks; the sympathy she feels for the individual employees and the love she experiences in relation to the larger team and their joint work.

In the many big and small teamwork relationships in the department, the continuous everyday flow of communication and work performances, the team develops a confidence in its own ability *not* to be ripped apart by internal conflicts or external pressures. The conflicts, cutbacks, setbacks and frustrations are all part of everyday working life – as are teamwork, supplementary grants and positive surprises. But the team can deal with all that. Britt knows that is part of working life, and that it is possible to solve problems and move past them. The more times the team experiences that problems can be solved, and conflicts can be settled, the better it gets at handling them. It is possible to learn from experience. Britt has learned that everyday life also includes conflicts, anger, hostility, jealousy and so forth, but she has also learned that it is an ordinary part of everyday working life. In the situation, these experiences may be worrying and give cause for concern, reflection, revised practices and altered relationships, but they are essentially unavoidable. Britt generally likes her staff, her work, the necessity and the room for personal expression the work also offers. Not passion, but not indifference either. Love based on necessity and everyday tasks.

We have sought to capture and describe three types of task-based love relationships: love of the creative opportunities for self-realisation, as exemplified by Vita. Love of the task comprised of a defence against difficult demands in other life domains and a parallel desire to create concrete changes, as exemplified by Jeff. And, finally, love of the task in the form of ordinary, down-to-earth love of a combination of the task and the co-workers that makes everything work from the perspective of everyday life. In all three cases, there is a love relationship between person and task. The task is libidinal. The task is crucial for the individual. The task contains an opportunity for self-realization as well as an opportunity for escape. The task offers an opportunity for healing 'inner worms' and repairing rather than repeating past traumas or unresolved experiences. The task may be libidinal because it is extraordinary and innovative, and it may be libidinal because it is mundane, continuous, meaningful and embedded in a greater community.

Love in the organization

The third and final perspective on love relationships in working life pertains to love of the organization or the team as a whole. We will look at the organization or the team as the object of the individual's love, and we will debate the organization's 'libidinal centre' as a way of defining and understanding psychological dynamics and relations and as a concept that embraces the diversity of love relations in working life.

We encounter many whose main love object in their working life is not so much an individual person or task but a more generalized love of the group they belong to or the organization they work for. As with love directed at the pair and the work task, we see both the passionate and the more rational and mundane. Naturally, it makes a difference that the love object is a group or an organization. These are larger units that contain numerous relations. However, it is no easy matter to determine whether they are more complex or place bigger demands on the ability to tolerate ambivalence, or whether it is wonderful or frustrating that there are so many potential libidinal objects. The point here is that a work team, a department, an organization can be an object of love in its own right. We connect and identify with the context we are a part of. That may be a specific and clearly defined unit: I am proud of working at the Sunny Side Nursing Home, we do a good job, and our residents really love being here. Or, I am pleased to be part of this particular consultancy team helping the municipal administration deal with the more vexing and complicating issues. It may also be a less clearly defined context: I love being part of the music industry, the projects I do with others are fun and meaningful, even if it can be tough at times. Or, I am a doctor, a member of the medical profession, with our professional ethics, quality standards and procedures.

Visholm uses the term 'giant subjects' (our translation) to refer to large systems that incorporate a sprawling and complex structure of sub-systems, but which are perceived as units we can have certain feelings and attitudes toward (Visholm, 1993). Examples of giant subjects include 'traffic,' 'the banks,' 'society' and 'Copenhageners,' and thus, the love may be directed at the organization as a giant subject. Employees may feel let down by an organization they regard with love when the organization acts in a way that the employees did not expect, perhaps thinking, 'I expected better from you.' The libido is withdrawn. As discussed above, love of the group, the organization or the profession/industry/field is closely interwoven with our sense of identity.

Love of the group and the organization

Workplaces are – ideally – meaningful communities to the employees which serve a purpose that is also meaningful to others. Examples include preschool teachers caring for children, legal experts involved in drawing up legislation or organizations in charge of building bridges and roads, preventing water or air pollution or delivering produce to shops and supermarkets. To some, participating in a workplace community, big or small, becomes a key identity factor, a love relationship: 'We at Novo Nordisk,' 'We at the Royal Danish Theatre,' 'We at Sunny Side Nursing Home.'

In 1921, Freud wanted to understand what made an individual give up, at least, parts of their identity and identify with the group (Freud, 1921/1955b, pp. 65–144). The echo from the First World War will still have been resonating, and Freud found that the individual's capacity to think seems to be inhibited (making the person more stupid, less reflective or less critical), making the person more inclined to be governed by the intensification of affects (ibid., p. 84) and generally less free in the group. He set out to understand what binds the individuals in the group together, and how this group identification can be conceptualized psychologically. He regards the nature of the group spirit as a love relationship and assumes that the *libido* is the power that holds the group together: 'and to what power could this feat be better ascribed than to Eros, which holds together everything in the world?' (ibid., p. 91). The mutual libidinal bind between the individuals in the group develops into a group identification in a community around a leader or a leading idea. Freud concludes that 'A primary group of this kind is a number of individuals who have put one and the same object in the place of their ego-ideal and have consequently identified themselves with one another in their ego' (ibid., p. 115). Our purpose here is not to achieve an understanding of group psychology, but of the love relationship between individual and organization, group or giant subject. What sort of object might supplant the individual's ego-ideal? We mentioned the ego-ideal earlier in this chapter as the component of the super-ego that contains the ideals and standards that the individual strives for. All that is good, right and beautiful. In an earlier publication we sought, with inspiration from the sociologist Norbert Elias, to define the concept of a we-ideal. The we-ideal represents the group's wishes, ambitions, dreams. What the group wants to be, what it strives for, and what it imagines it could become (Bonnerup & Hasselager, 2008, p. 234). In the present context we do not address the dynamics of the we-ideal in a group. However, based on this concept and Freud's analysis we propose that the individual gives up or replaces (parts of) their ego-ideal with a we-ideal, imagined or perceived. That the individual identifies with and in a sense becomes 'Novo Nordisk,' 'The Royal Danish Theatre' or 'Sunny Side Nursing Home.' That is not just a way of being, it is a way of belonging.

We all carry experiences with us from the first group we belonged to: our family. These experiences influence our perception of groups. Are they threatening, dangerous, creative or pleasant? Is it possible to be oneself – alone, in the presence of others? Or is it impossible? Will we associate being alone in a group with being lonely? As countless writers have pointed out over the ages, love is a complex phenomenon. Love of a group or an organization often implies complex and complicated emotions such as envy or hate. The opposite of love is something akin to indifference and apathy. We may feel love toward a group that we find it exceedingly difficult to be part of.

Love can grow and express itself in temporary groups, almost like being in love. Taking part in a summer camp is a good example. The entire world unfolds inside the group and the camp setting, and for the duration of the camp, everything else fades into the background. Similarly, in a longer course or project, the entire class or team may be embraced with love by all the individual members for the duration of the course or the project. Once the course or the project is over, parting can be painful. Post-project blues. The class or group lives on inside us, as recollections, emotions, urges, moods. Sometimes we delay the parting by agreeing to stay in touch, but once everyone has returned home, other engagements soon move into the foreground, while the reunion day that was arranged slips into the background and loses some of its vibrancy. Afterwards, some might wonder why it was that they were *so* excited about that particular group.

Libido is invested in a group, and when the group reaches the end of its lifespan, in real or perceived terms, the libido has to be withdrawn. It is associated with some degree of sadness to note that the group no longer exists. Either because the task has been completed. Or because it is necessary to leave the group. When the group membership is severed, the individual has to let go of the projections attributed to them. Welcome as well as unwelcome projections. The person has to give up a role that may have had certain qualities that it feels difficult to give up. Love of the group may be perceived as impressions, sensations and situations that can be difficult to leave behind. Not just projections. It can be difficult to determine whether it is love of the individuals – some more than others – the group as a whole, the task the group handles or the potential it possesses (just imagine what we might become). The love may be directed at the actual group or at the 'group in the mind.'

Companies that are in a crisis or are receiving unfavourable press coverage may find that the employees' solidarity with the organization waxes and wanes. For employees who are otherwise loyal to the company, an intended or perceived sleight can cause them to withdraw the libido they have invested in the company. This is not only because it becomes difficult to see oneself as part of the company; to some, the experience feels almost as if the company had betrayed them or committed adultery or embezzlement, and they feel let down by the organization.

This may be personified by management. Or it may be perceived as if it is the workplace as such that has failed, that the giant subject has let them down. From being idealized, it is now devalued. Football teams that unexpectedly lose, companies that fall behind in the competition, departments that are compelled by the circumstances to change course or goals risk having the staff withdraw their libido and their attachment to the organization as a whole. The recent, controversial Danish school reform probably led to many discussions at family events if there were school teachers or head masters/mistresses present – or both groups at once. The Danish Tax Agency and the seemingly endless stories of mismanagement and the loss of huge amounts of revenue. Preschools that become front-page news due to reports of neglect. Love can turn to indifference. Who cares! Love of a group or an organization may take many different forms. In the following case story, we meet a leadership team where love of the group for a while became the factor that made it possible to overcome the difficulties they were facing.

The leadership team at Old Mill School

Old Mill School is a large primary and lower secondary school in a city. Owen has been the director of the school for about ten years. There have been many major ups and downs over the years, lots of challenges to deal with. School mergers, school reform, working-hours reform, budget cuts and the inclusion of children with special needs. These challenges have been accompanied by internal conflicts and HR issues as well as solutions and dedication, celebrations and many big and small events in the school's life. Lots of challenges, lots of work. A teaching staff where many of the teachers have been with the school for many years. Competent, solid, experienced, but also with clear opinions about what sort of leadership Owen ought to provide, and what decisions he should make. But also, younger team members who bring in new inspiration and a readiness to take on the many projects that they were involved in as part of the wider municipal development strategy. A growing number of teachers were feeling under pressure and had difficulty keeping up, and over the past few years, sick leave due to stress had increased sharply; another major challenge. A challenge for the individual teachers afflicted with stress, for the continuity and quality of teaching, for the budget. The school board was a mixed lot. Some parents understood the challenges the school and Owen were facing and offered relevant support, while others seemed to be motivated to serve on the board because it gave them influence over which teachers would teach the class their own child attended; the latter were generally quick to criticize Owen and the teachers in no uncertain terms if they got the chance. Owen was generally on good terms with the municipal administration, but he felt that it was hard to keep up. So many projects, ideas, interdisciplinary learning environments, development initiatives. It was a real struggle to find time for everything and to prioritize among the many tasks. He was constantly falling behind, struggling to keep up. Owen worked hard, but even he got tired sometimes. In addition to Owen, the school's leadership team comprised four departmental heads, one of whom had been the director of a school that had closed down. That had caused some awkwardness at first – once they were equals, but now, Owen was in charge. After six months or so, the awkwardness had faded away, and they now got on well. There had been a few changes in the leadership team over the past ten years. They had been necessary to make sure the team could handle and adapt to the new leadership tasks that accompanied the many changes. Sometimes, that had led to difficult times and conflicts, especially three to four years ago, when he had to let a leader go who could not live up to the requirements of modern school leadership. That had been emotionally taxing, both for the person who was let go and for Owen and the rest of the team. By now, they had put all that behind them. For a couple of years, the team had been stable and increasingly effective. They had managed to establish and develop a fundamentally trusting atmosphere, where they were usually able to listen, debate, disagree and appreciate one another. On a personal level, they were quite different, but they shared key values, and they all had great mutual respect for each other. Sure, there were days when things were difficult, and Owen felt that he had to go out of his way to accommodate a member of the leadership team. Or that a disagreement took far too long to sort out. But basically, he felt that he was being seen, supported and respected by his subordinate leaders, and he knew that they felt the same way about him and about each other. That was good, but the school director's job was also exhausting, and sometimes thankless. Occasionally, he thought about throwing in the towel when he had come home late several days in row, when parents rang him to complain, or when the municipal administration had once again launched a project with an unreasonably tight deadline. It wore him down – and was it really worth it? However, he knew for sure that if he left Old Mill School for another school, he would at best face different problems, not smaller or fewer ones. He knew that the leadership team he had built was exceptional. That was the source of his energy.

Owen decided to stay at Old Mill School because he basically thrived in his job. His love of the leadership team endured and remained a key factor in that decision. He knew that he might swop one set of problems for a slightly different set of problems, but he also knew that an effective and trusting team was not to be taken for granted. For Owen, the leadership team was also the libidinal centre of his working life. In the final section of the chapter, we will take a closer look at that concept.

The libidinal centre

Organizations have a main task, a leadership, a structure, routines, competences and deliverables. The main task in particular occupies a central role as the organization's core, its raison d'être. We are inspired by Simons Western's thinking about the libidinal centre in the organization (Western, 2016). It is not a fixed and fully developed concept, but rather a concept we think enables new perspectives on love and life in the organization. In 'the libidinal centre,' it is not necessarily the main task as such that is the main issue. The libidinal centre is the place where thoughts, feelings, commitment go and are expressed; it is the special contexts where it seems most attractive to be involved – 'where it's at,' or where the most committed members engage in work in a way that makes them forget about time and place. The processes may be creative and innovative, or they may resemble play and still go far beyond play. The libidinal centre may also be the arena of power struggles that the individual members are deeply engaged in.

The libidinal centre is something other and more than the meaningfulness of the work. It is attractive, enjoyable or profoundly necessary, but it does not direct attention away from the tasks or the organizational reality. It is not characterized by indifference, apathy, neutrality. It is libidinal in the sense that libido is a vital drive directed at organizational objects, processes and structures. Above all, the libidinal centre is an emotional investment, it defines the direction and character of the commitment. The libidinal centre is an imagined and perceived space. However, it does take place, and people do get together, also in a physical space where they feel, alone or with others, that they are all involved in something important related to the task and the organization. An example of a physical space that forms the setting of a libidinal centre could be the teachers' lounge, which in many schools is, or has been, an iconic space where important processes, decisions, conflicts and love relationship play out.

We imagine that the libidinal centre in an organization is neither a fully individual nor a fully collective phenomenon. There will be several places where the libido can converge and be condensed, and which in that sense constitute a centre. The director of the municipality's technical and environmental administration and the gardener responsible for planting spring flowers in city squares do not necessarily have a shared libidinal centre, even though they work within the same organization. For the director, that centre may be the leadership team where important decisions are made and important power struggles play out. However, it may also be a cross-municipal and cross-disciplinary project that has the potential to set new standards for the integration of environmental and traffic-safety concerns. For the gardener, it may be the work during those weeks in the month of May when everything grows and blooms. Or the team she works in. Or a special collaboration with the Botanical Garden, where they play with new plants, experiment and take chances. Together with others, the two will find a libidinal centre here and now. Having an awareness of the convergence of libido in an organization can help shed light on seemingly irrational processes, on spaces for especially creative and developing processes and on entrenched barriers to organizational development.

In the case story about Sandra and Martin and their 'mission impossible,' the assignment they were handed as a pair is an obvious candidate for a libidinal centre. The project was invested with many emotions from many different sides, and some fairly destructive dynamics were playing out around the pair. With Luke and Mia, whom we introduced as the playful creative par, it seems obvious to imagine that their particular collaboration was their libidinal centrum, albeit not in the same destructive manner as with Sandra and Martin. At Food for Fridays, the libidinal centre during the initial phase of the organization's life was Vittorio and Laura's kitchen table, where many ideas were hatched, and decisions were made. For a time, the director's office was a libidinal centre, where points of view were exchanged, chances were taken, tears were shed, and conflicts took form. Later, the meetings came to lack libido, perhaps due to unresolved power struggles or decisions that were delayed. For some time, Ethan and Fabio's friendship was a libidinal centre and a setting for passion, energy, optimism and conflicts.

Closing remarks

We have covered a wide range of topics in our effort to understand and define the concept of love in organizations. We have attempted to build a psychological basis for understanding love, leaning especially on psychoanalysis to compile elements for a definition of love as a concept and a phenomenon. We have discussed the concept of libido, a traditional psychoanalytic concept. We have introduced concept of perceptive identification, which makes a new and inspiring supplement to the traditional concepts of projection and projective identification and the traditional understanding overall. From here, we moved on to explore love in working life under three headings: love in working-life pairs, love of the task and, finally, love of the group or the organization.

The perspective of love has many potential implications for practice that are worth considering. What is the impact for organizations, where relations in many ways become the central structure because the organizational chart keeps changing? What does it mean when many close working relations are broken up, and tasks are reconfigured? Where do the inner worms and their holes go to be translated to creative work or destructive processes? What pairs are formed and become significant, and what impact does that have for the organizations? Where might the libidinal centres find their place?

References

Andersen, K. L. (2010). Venskabsgrupper. In Å. Lading & B. Aa. Jørgensen (Eds.), *Grupper – om kollektivets bevidste og ubevidste dynamikker* (p. 2). Copenhagen, Denmark: Frydenlund.
Armstrong, D., & Rustin, M. (2015). *Social defences against anxiety*. London, UK: Karnac.
Badiou, A. (2015). *Lovprisning af kærligheden*. Århus, Denmark: Forlaget Philosophia.
Binney, G., Wilke, G., & Williams, C. (2003). *Leaders in transition. The dramas of ordinary heroes*. Berkhamsted, UK: Ashridge.

Bick, E. (1968). The experience of skin. *International Journal of Psycho-analysis*, 49, 484–486.
Bion, W. (1968). *Experiences in groups*. London, UK: Tavistock.
Bollas, C. (1987). *The shadow of the object. Psychoanalysis of the unthought known*. New York, NY: Columbia University Press.
Bollas, C. (2007). *The Freudian moment*. London, UK: Karnac.
Bonnerup, B., & Hasselager, A. (2008). *Gruppen på arbejde*. Copenhagen, Denmark: Hans Reitzels Forlag.
Bonnerup, B., & Hasselager, A. (2011). Ledelse af læreprocesser i grupper. In P. Helth (Ed.), *Ledelse og læring i praksis*. Copenhagen, Denmark: Forlaget Samfundslitteratur.
Brinkmann, S. (2011). Følelser på godt og ondt. In C. Elmholdt, & L. Tanggaard (Eds.), *Følelser i ledelse*. Århus, Denmark: Klim.
Buechler, S. (2011). Someone to watch over me. In B. Willock (Ed.), *Loneliness and longing. Conscious and unconscious aspects*. London, UK: Routledge.
Csikszentmihalyi, M. (1990). *Flow. The psychology of optimal experience*. New York, NY: Harper & Row.
Dalal, F. (2002). *Race, colour and the process of racialization*. London, UK: Routledge.
Damasio, A. (2012). *Self comes to mind*. New York, NY: Pantheon.
Demandante, D. (2014). Lacanian perspectives on love. *Kritike*, 8(1), 102–118.
Elmholdt, C., & Tanggaard, L. (2011). *Følelser i ledelse*. Århus, Denmark: Klim.
Fineman, S. (2003). *Understanding emotion at work*. London, UK: Sage.
French, R. (2007). Friendship and organization: Learning from the Western friendship tradition. *Management and Organizational History*, 2, 255–272.
French, R., Gosling, J., & Case, P. (2009). Betrayal and friendship. *Society and Business Review*, 4(2), 146–158.
Freud, S. (1955b). Beyond the pleasure principle, group psychology and other works. In J. Strachey (Ed. and Trans.), *The standard edition of the complete psychological works of Sigmund Freud (Vol. 18)*. London, UK: Hogarth. (Original work published 1920–1922).
Fromm, E. (1956). *The art of loving*. New York, NY: Harper & Brothers.
Gabriel, Y. (1999). *Organizations in depth*. London, UK: Sage.
Halton, W., & Sprince, J. (2016). Oscillating images. Perceptions of couples in organizations. In A. Novakovic (Ed.), *Couple dynamics. Psychoanalytical perspectives in work with the individual, the couple and the group*. London, UK: Karnac.
Heinskou, T., & Visholm, S. (2004). *Psykodynamisk organisationspsykologi. På arbejde under overfladen*. Copenhagen, Denmark: Hans Reitzels Forlag.
Hirschhorn, L. (2001). *Passion and group life. Examining moments of creativity and destructiveness*. CFAR. www.cfar.com.
Hirschhorn, L. (2003). *Reworking authority. Leading and following in the post-modern organization*. Cambridge, MA: MIT Press.
Hochschild, A. R. (1997). *The time bind: When work becomes home and home becomes work*. New York, NY: Metropolitan Books.
Holst, J. (2015). *Venskab. Det gode mellem mennesker*. Århus, Denmark: Århus Universitetsforlag.
Højbjerg, H. (2005). Hermeneutik. In L. Fuglsang & P. Bitsch Olsen (Eds), *Videnskabsteori i samfundsvidenskaberne*. Copenhagen, Denmark: Roskilde Universitetsforlag.
Illouz, E. (2007). *Cold intimacies. The making of emotional capitalism*. Cambridge, UK: Polity Press.

Jakobsen, P., & Visholm, S. (1987). *Parforholdet*. Copenhagen, Denmark: Politisk Revy.
Karpatschof, B., & Katzenelson, B. (2011). *Klassisk og moderne psykologisk teori*. Copenhagen, Denmark: Hans Reitzels Forlag.
Kernberg, O. F. (1995). *Love relations. Normality and pathology*. New Haven, CT: Yale University Press.
Miller, E. J., & Rice, K. A. (1975). Selections from: Systems of organizations. In A. D. Colman & H. Bexton (Eds), *Group relations reader 1*. Washington, DC: A. K. Rice Institute.
Nettleton, S. (2017). *The metapsychology of Christopher Bollas. An Introduction*. London, UK/New York, NY: Routledge.
Novakovic, A. (Ed.) (2016). *Couple dynamics. Psychoanalytical perspectives in work with the individual, the couple and the group*. London, UK: Karnac.
Olsen, O. A. (Ed.) (2002). *Psykodynamisk leksikon*. Copenhagen, Denmark: Gyldendal.
Olsen, O. A., & Køppe, S. (1981). *Freuds psykoanalyse*. Copenhagen, Denmark: Gyldendal.
Paahus, A. (2013). *Kærlighed*. Århus, Denmark: Århus Universitetsforlag.
Senge, P. M. (1990). *The fifth discipline*. New York, NY: Doubleday.
Sievers, B. (1993). Motivation as invention. In *Work, death and life itself. Essays on management and organization*. Berlin, Germany/New York, NY: Walter de Gruyter.
Stern, D. (1985). *The interpersonal world of the infant*. New York, NY: Basic Books.
Sundhedsstyrelsen (2009). *Sundhed og trivsel på arbejdspladsen – Inspiration til systematisk og strategisk arbejde med sundhedsfremme i virksomheden*. Copenhagen, Denmark: Sundhedsstyrelsen, Center for Forebyggelse.
Visholm, S. (1993). *Overflade og dybde*. Copenhagen, Denmark: Forlaget Politisk Revy.
Visholm, S. (2001). *Om læring og psykodynamik*. Unpublished draft.
Western, S. (2016). Personal communication.
Winnicott, D. (1971). *Playing and reality*. London, UK: Tavistock.
Winnicott, D. (1986). *Home is where we start from*. London, UK: Penguin.

Online sources

Freud, S. (1885). Letter to Martha Bernays. 21 Oct. www.freud.org.uk/about/faq.

Chapter 3

Loneliness

Our working life is a source of and a setting for relationships, community, shared efforts and, as discussed in the previous chapter, friendships and other important loving relationships. However, our working life is also, and perhaps precisely for that reason, a setting for profound loneliness. That is the second theme of the book and our main focus in this second main chapter. Many people feel lonely. We experience this in our practice, and we see it documented in population studies (e.g., Lasgaard & Friis, 2014, 2015). Loneliness is not necessarily readily apparent. A person may have a family, friends, a social life, a workplace and co-workers and, in many cases, perceived meaningful work. But many of the people we meet feel lonely in important parts or aspects of their personal and working lives. Lonely in their formal role as managers, mid-level managers or top executives. Lonely in their professional role as, for example, specialist, chief surgeon, occupational therapist, economist and so forth. Lonely in their particular view of the organization – lonely with a major responsibility, as the only person who carries the full history of the organization, the only one to feel obligated by a set of decisions. Or lonely because they stand out due to their personal characteristics, values or opinions. The only woman, the only Asian, the only person over 60 or 30 years of age, the only single person. Lonely because they are not *fully* included in the workplace community. Lonely because they feel left out, without anyone really noticing it. Lonely because they are different, isolated; lonely because they hold themselves to too high a standard and thus shut others out. The website of the Danish mental health foundation Psykiatrifonden writes the following about loneliness:

> Many feel lonely because they do not share their feelings and thoughts with others out of fear that others will either fail to understand or consider them strange or out of place. Many are relieved to discover that their thoughts and feelings really aren't all that dangerous or strange, once they have said them out loud.
> (www.psykiatrifonden.dk; our translation)

Loneliness has many sources and paths. And loneliness is real.

Loneliness can be a new and surprising experience or a loyal, if troubling, lifelong companion. Some understand their loneliness, others are perplexed by it. Some people's loneliness we can understand, while that of others seems perplexing. Why that person? Why now? Why in this situation? In our treatment of the second main theme of the book we first examine and define the phenomenon of loneliness and demonstrate why we think it is important to address the issue of loneliness in an organizational context. We look at loneliness in both a contemporary and a historical context, and we look at loneliness from a theoretical perspective. We then go on to look at loneliness as it appears in various areas of working life.

The phenomenon of loneliness

Why is the concept of loneliness relevant? And why now?

Loneliness is not a new invention. From history we know of hermits, pilgrims, monastic life and meditative retreats, people seeking solitude for life or for a period, often with a religious ambition of moving closer to the divine. We also know it from literature, both fiction and poetry. Being stranded on a desert island is a widespread and well-described phantasy that has given rise to many a yarn, from tales of horror and despair to stories of hedonistic idyll. In his book *Kunsten at være alene* [The art of being alone] the Danish Professor of Psychology Peter Elsass examines and describes loneliness through the lens of psychology, theology and literature to approach an understanding of what he calls 'the good form of loneliness' (Elsass, 2016; our translation). Loneliness can be perceived in many different ways and have different qualities in a person's life.

Loneliness in our current network society appears to be associated with feelings of both shame and guilt. In our individualized (Western) world, the prevailing motto is that the individual is essentially responsible for shaping their own destiny. If you are lonely, it is up to you to get off the sofa and do something about it. Nevertheless, many of the people we meet in our practice live and grapple with loneliness in different forms. Most people are reluctant to share these experiences and feelings with others. We now know that long-term loneliness is associated with increased mortality (Lasgaard & Friis, 2014, 2015). We also know that just under 5% of the adult population in Denmark feel very lonely. Among young people, the figure is even higher (ibid.). Studies show clear correlation between loneliness and a number of social factors. Being single, having no attachment to the labour market and/or having no or limited education are the biggest risk factors for perceived loneliness (ibid.). The same studies point out the scarcity of research on loneliness; it is easy to see this as a reflection of the taboo generally surrounding the loneliness.

Loneliness is a subjective experience, but it is something other and more than that. We cannot think our way out of loneliness, nor can we necessarily act our way out. Loneliness is perceived and experienced, loneliness can be part of working life, a necessary part of a role or a task or an unwanted experience of being excluded or being unable to fit into the corporate culture. Loneliness is a group phenomenon, and perhaps the experience of loneliness is at least as painful in the company of others as in solitary retreat. Loneliness means being involuntarily cut off from perceived, imagined or actual relations, here and now or in the long term.

Loneliness and 'homo sentimentalis'

In her book *Cold intimacies – the making of emotional capitalism* (Illouz, 2007), the Israeli sociologist Eva Illouz offers an interesting analysis of the advent of psychology in working life; an analysis that contributes to our understanding of loneliness and the shame that surrounds it. Illouz points to a development that began in the mid 20th century, when emotions went from being a strictly internal, personal phenomenon to moving into the centre of both the self and our social life. Emotions are communicated, articulated, prioritized. Illouz describes this new emphasis on emotions in social life as the rise of 'homo sentimentalis,' emotional man, and she argues that both men and women have become increasingly emotionally androgynous during the course of the 20th century. Boys are allowed to cry, and girls are allowed to be angry. Briefly put, our personality is the key to success – socially, as a leader and career-wise. We see this manifested, for example, in the interest in personal leadership, the use of personality testing in recruiting and the general interest in and spread of psychology, including organizational psychology, that gained momentum in the mid 20th century, especially over the past 20–30 years. Illouz points to three factors that made this development possible: the economic growth we saw during the second half of the 20th century, the wider spread of therapy and the women's liberation movement (ibid.).

Illouz is not alone in taking a critical view of social developments over the course of the past century. Other writers and scholars have pointed out how methods of control in working life are becoming increasingly sophisticated and pervasive. First, the emphasis was on controlling the human body (scientific management), next, social relations (human relations), then the intellect (human resource) and finally our emotions, spirit, values, so that the capitalists/owners could maximize the workers'/employees' productivity. This criticism is found, for example, in certain manifestations of work psychology (Volpert 1980; Petersen & Sabroe, 1984); in the Frankfurt School, it is represented, for example, by Nielsen and Nielsen (1978). Sennett critiques contemporary trends in his book *The corrosion of character* (Sennett, 1998), and Gareth Morgan's book *Images of organizations* documents the historical development of non-explicit notions of organizations through an illustrative discussion of various organizational metaphors (Morgan, 2006).

Illouz argues that the introduction of the psychological discourse 'democratizes' or loosens up the power relations between management and staff – and that this trend comes at a cost. Psychology becomes relevant not only because it offers an understanding of challenges in modern and postmodern (working) life; as a scientific discipline, psychology also introduces discourses that contribute to creating the problems and challenges we experience. Illouz points out that the humanistic movement in psychology from around the 1950s offered a less deterministic view of personality: personal change is possible. Self-actualization, self-realization, therapy and personal insight defined the 'royal road' to good mental health. She points out how the language and mindset of therapy have come to permeate our thinking about and understanding of self, relations and the problems and challenges we encounter in working life. Illouz highlights that the interviews conducted in the famous Hawthorne Studies bear a striking resemblance to the therapeutic interview (Illouz, 2007). She describes the 20th-century approach to problems as a *therapeutic emotional style*. However, the grand narrative of self-development, insight, therapy and self-help is also a narrative of suffering. Illouz writes,

> Because psychology's principal vocation has been to alleviate a variety of forms of psychic suffering through an undefined ideal of help and self-realization and because the therapeutic persuasion has in fact contributed to the creation of a personal memory of suffering, it ironically creates much of the suffering it is supposed to alleviate.
>
> (ibid., p. 62)

The notion that personal change is possible thus also implies the notion of suffering that necessitates change, the notion that suffering can (should) be addressed as an opportunity for personal development, and that improvement is our own individual responsibility. Problems and maladaptive personality features become a challenge that can – and should be – addressed. Ultimately, the individual is responsible for their own health and happiness. Unhappiness is thus further exacerbated, because it is our own responsibility – unhappiness is a personal failure. This, combined with the tendency to understand happiness as the absence of suffering, threatens to exacerbate the burden. The narrative of self-development and self-realization thus contributes to the emergence of loneliness. 'It's your own fault ....'

The therapeutic mindset finds its way (unseen) into our organizations. Psychology, including organizational psychology, gains momentum from the 1980s and becomes relevant because it offers an understanding of challenges in postmodern life. Clearly, the therapeutic mindset contributes to management's focus on the fact that the members of the organization are living people who should be perceived and treated as such. That is inherently sensible and desirable and more *humane* than viewing the employees as machines or components in the production apparatus with no rights or autonomy (a view that still prevails in large parts of the world). Authority figures are encouraged to understand, reflect on and act with reason and insight when they exercise power in relations. Authority figures are encouraged to base their perceptions and treatment of their employees on insight into communication, motivation, relations and personality psychology. Insight into the importance of relations, education and change psychology, for example, ranges from insight into employees as human beings to insight into coaching, question and conversation techniques that stem mainly from therapeutic insight and methods. Neurological patterns, neural networks and mirror neurons have become a source of knowledge about human beings. That leads to insight but also gives rise to new management and control technologies, as described by several critical voices, including the Danish sociologist Rasmus Willig (Willig, 2016).

However, in addition to acting as a management and control technology, it also reflects and contributes to the development of human technology of the self. Gaining insight into deep-seated human motivations can potentially lead to a demand to get those motivations under control. If you are struggling with insecure attachment, you have to learn to become more secure in your attachment or turn your insecurity into an asset. That is both potentially invasive and helpful. It becomes invasive if it means that certain variants of normality are pathologized: you should not have those feelings – get rid of them. It is helpful if it means that everyday setbacks become reality-oriented; not as something we need to defend ourselves against but as something we have to learn to deal with, live with, maybe get help to live with. Help to understand our reactions and to integrate new elements and let go of what was lost.

Positive thinking and loneliness

From the 1960s onwards and, in our assessment, especially in the 21st century, the therapeutic style makes it into everyday human relationships, from collegial relations or relations between managers and staff to our social and personal relations. Emotions not only exist (and may need to be controlled); they should also find a relevant expression. In recent years with the added twist that inconvenient emotions can, must and should be dealt with and turned into creative and, ideally, positive emotions (see, e.g. Willig, 2016). One of the many consequences of this trend is that it exacerbates the experience of loneliness because it may give the individual the impression that they are the only person struggling with 'inappropriate' emotions, and because it seems difficult or impossible to share experiences of inappropriate emotions.

In his 2016 book, Willig offers a vivid description of how a focus on positive thinking as the only legitimate mindset marginalizes the individual's experiences of working life and its conditions and generally undermines organizations, causing them to lose a crucial capacity for critical thinking (ibid.). "I am fed up.

I'm not allowed to be fed up. I have to be something other than fed up. I'm the only one who doesn't know how not to be fed up. I can't talk to anyone about the fact that I'm fed up, or that I find it hard to stop being fed up, because I'm not even allowed to be fed up. And if I say that I'm fed up, I'll infect the others, and I can't. And I can't talk to anyone about the fact that I can't talk about being fed up, and that I can't stop being fed up."

That is, more or less, how an inner monologue might sound, a dialogue that does not really make the person any less fed up or promotes their understanding of what reasons *exist* or *do not exist* to be fed up (replace 'fed up' with 'angry,' 'sad,' 'happy' or whatever seems most interesting; the exercise is the same). Willig has also offered important points to help us understand what we will later discuss as 'the fear of disclosure.' He argues that the criticism that previously took an external direction, targeted at society, working conditions, employers and structural and economic conditions, has now made a 180 degree turn and is instead directed inward, as self-criticism. Economic and political conditions that should rightfully be targeted escape criticism, and instead we remain ever critical of ourselves and our performances, feeling that we are personally responsible for developing and improving ourselves. We could get an earlier start, eat healthier, work harder, run farther, develop more. He mentions the fitness wave, coaching and a constant focus on self-development as examples of management and control instruments that are far more serious and far-reaching than we might think, and which direct the criticism inward, at the individual, who could always do better, be more adaptable, be fitter. One of Willig's books (Willig, 2013) has the very illustrative title *Kritikkens U-vending* (The U turn of criticism) in a snappy retort to Scharmer's book on Theory U (Scharmer, 2007).

The power of the demand for positivity as a control and management instrument is that it is a perfect match for our super-ego. Perfectly suited to join the super-ego's list of requirements, imperatives and prohibitions. Initially in the form of promises of improvement and success: you will be happier, thrive and develop, live longer. Next, in the form of imperatives: you must be happier, thrive and develop, live longer. Ultimately, in punitive terms: it is your own fault if you are not happy, if you fail to thrive and develop, if you do not live longer. The internalized requirements of perfection and of taking charge of one's own happiness, success and health exacerbate loneliness. I am all alone with (my super-ego and) the demands I place on myself, and I worry about being exposed as a failure. My fear of exposure feeds my experience of loneliness.

When the annual 'employee development conversation' was introduced in Denmark, there were some critical voices: what a waste of time! Who can offer advice on how to do this? Isn't that just another HR stunt? Can't we just address the problems when they arise? Those were the sorts of questions that were raised. Today, these conversations are a recurring element in most HR development repertoires. Many organizations, big and small, also have arrangements with crisis psychology centres and stress coaches to provide support for employees in need. That is obviously a help for many, but it also instructs the employee to recover (hopefully quickly). Regardless of the pros and cons, it represents a therapeutic style that is finding its way into, is practised in and contributes to shaping relations in organizations.

Everyday setbacks

Another angle on the phenomenon of loneliness is the potential pathologization of everyday variations on normality. At the risk of being banal: we all know that setbacks are an unavoidable part of life. One person cannot have children, another has more than they want. Mr/Miss Right fails to materialize and is replaced by others in a series of monogamous relationships of a finite duration. 'Till death do you part' has a less absolute expiration date. Children who fail to thrive, inheritances that are not distributed as one had hoped – *I* was supposed to get the old coffeepot or the 12 million Euro, but that's not how it turned out. Promotions and work tasks are not always justly distributed. That's life.

Sometimes, everyday crises turn into – or are turned into – incidents that require treatment. We have institutions dedicated to helping divorced parents, preschools have contingency plans for family breakups, and even nursing schools might have personal development plans for the kids. Could you do things differently? Could the child engage in slightly more relevant play and thus achieve an optimal development course? Coaching for children, parenting courses. It appears to be extremely difficult to make it through life a normal person without receiving expert assistance to handle setbacks and new demands. That *may* be helpful, but it may also be a way to pathologize normal, everyday problems. A professionalization of assistance to completely normal setbacks. Pathologizing and professionalizing assistance with normal setbacks feeds the individual's loneliness. Here I am, a new mother, a recent dentistry graduate or a newly appointed CEO – all alone, with big, vexing challenges, and I feel paralysed. My challenges are treated very seriously by consultants and other experts. Might it sometimes be simpler and less lonely if we could simply talk to a colleague or knock on a neighbour's door, maybe find that someone else is facing the same standard-issue burdensome and life-altering problems? The tendency to seek help to 'recover' can become an indirect denial of pain and irreparable loss. That leads to loneliness. Because the individual is not seen. Experience is ignored. Experience is pushed out.

Being someone 'special'

In parallel with the application of the therapeutic mindset to working-life relations we see another trend, which is often referred to as individualization. The individual takes centre stage in society. The family has to adapt to the individual rather than the other way around, there has to be room for everyone's personal self-realization project. The trend has been documented and analysed convincingly by several leading sociologists, including Beck (1992) and Giddens (1990, 1991). A general trend toward the perception that 'everyone shapes their own destiny,' from individuals to private companies or public-sector organizations. In the early 2010s, Professor Ove Kaj Pedersen at the Copenhagen Business School released a much-debated book describing the development from welfare state to competition state (Pedersen, 2011). While the welfare state aimed to create equality among the citizens of a country, the purpose of the competition state is to maximize the utility of the individual's labour potential, in part and especially by emphasizing the individual's own responsibility. That competition as a part of working life is hardly breaking news. A person may – as has probably always been the case – compete with themselves and everyone else, also within a team. The team is (also) in competition with similar teams within the same organization, just as the organization competes with other, similar organizations. Pedersen's book is sometimes portrayed as applauding increased competition, but in fact it is a descriptive analysis of a trend in society toward a growing emphasis on the individual and individual responsibility.

Individualization and the competition state are ways of describing and conceptualizing the mantra of constant change: YOU can do better! The individual comes to perceive this as a demand (and for most people a necessary and attractive drive) to be someone 'special' or to be perceived as such. To stand out from the crowd as the unique and special individual the person aims to be perceived as. It is not enough to be someone special; one has to be special in a particularly positive way. To be number one, the person who adds what is not already present. It is not attractive to be an anonymous foot soldier in the organization, a generic clerk, a mid-level manager among other mid-level managers and so forth; it is important to be whatever one is in a particularly positive and qualified way. This trend has both benefits and drawbacks. It lets us be seen as individuals, recognized as unique persons who excel at something. However, the competition and optimization mindset also produce losers. Someone has to be the least efficient, the slowest, the dumbest, since by definition, we cannot all be above average. Some of us have to be the ones who do not add anything unique but merely do our work and fulfil our role in the organization; good co-workers, stable employees, but not unique. When everybody wants to be special, paradoxically, uniqueness becomes commonplace. The ones who don't want to be special are the truly special ones.

Loneliness in the workplace

Managers are usually aware of their own role-based loneliness, the fact that they are alone in many contexts by virtue of their role. There is some knowledge they have to keep to themselves, contexts where they cannot cut loose (the annual Christmas party, for example), jokes they cannot tell and worries they cannot share with the employees, even if they are their closest day-to-day workmates. That is in itself a burden for many. But it makes sense. Sometimes, solitude turns to loneliness. The many surveys and assessments, cf. the competition paradigm and the evaluation society, can make individuals take a particularly critical look at their own performance. However, employees, including employees who appear to have good social relations and a good collegial network, can also feel quite alone.

There is growing pressure on the collegial community. Collegial relations have never been a simple matter, but the conditions for the workplace community are changing, and that gives rise to new difficulties. In our opinion, conflicts with co-workers and disagreements with supervisors carry a new level of vulnerability, as if disagreement has become more difficult to handle. Organizational structures, hierarchies and top-down management are replaced and supplemented with more fluid relations, self-management, network organization and continuous change. Organizations no longer offer security against the dissolution of the collegial or larger work-related network, as structural changes lead to changing relations, and because the networks are, in a sense, 'thinning,' becoming less based on joint work performance and shared experiences and more dependent on the quality and emotionality of relationships. It takes time to disagree properly, and it takes time to agree properly – or to move past the disagreement in a good way – and that time is rarely available. That in itself tends to make conflicts thinner and more individualized. The collegial community can be a straitjacket, a rigid hierarchy with strict norms, but the loss of community also means a loss of a network where the individual, if nothing else, at least had a validated position.

The German sociologist Hartmut Rosa offers a critique of late modern society that is relevant to our understanding of loneliness. In addition to the competition aspect, which Rosa, like Pedersen, has a critical assessment of, he studies the way we manage time and space in late modern society, and how alienation and acceleration affect today's society. Time is a scarce resource, at least for anyone with a place in the ever-accelerating labour market, with its constant requirement of increasing efficiency. We adapt to this constant acceleration and may gain by having many momentary experiences but lose out because we have fewer deep and genuine relational experiences (Rosa, 2010, pp. 41 ff.). As work relations and contexts become more fleeting, our ability to create, maintain and manage important relations comes under pressure. Relations do not last long enough to become significant as we survive or overcome difficulties together, through shared joy over joint tasks that are finally completed. Long-term relations have fewer opportunities for thriving. It may seem more natural to walk out, move on, rather than to stay and insist on developing a relationship, since it is going to be temporary anyway, because it is individual and contextual and not tied into ordinary working life or an unavoidable consequence of the work tasks. Abandoning a relationship or leaving an organization or a department also means that one person is left with something, while the other person left with something that may belong to the relationship, the task, the team or the organization, not to the individual. The problem does not go away but crops up in the next relationship.

A result of the dismantling of the organizational bureaucracy is that the individual no longer has a well-defined role or task portfolio to refer to. That may produce a sense of freedom and an opportunity to make one's work one's own. However, it can also highlight or produce organizational loneliness: does one really belong anywhere? Where? And why? There is rich opportunity for – and, perhaps especially, expectations of – being pushy and forming new contacts, but there is also a risk of making a wrong step, being excluded and slipping into oblivion. Anyone not busy building their own life, self-risks being overlooked.

There is an inherent risk that the technologies of self, with all their focus on emotions, become self-referencing technologies where the individual is both unnecessarily self-absorbed and left to fend for themselves. Working life, too, has to be something special, organizations need to compete and distinguish themselves, everything and everybody must be above average. Without sufficient focus on providing basic services, teaching children and looking after the elderly, performing one task after another, we risk losing focus on everyday life in the organization. For many, everyday life consists in a working life that includes co-workers, some easier to get along with than others, tasks to be completed and, of course, a pay cheque to take home.

Much has been written about the development of organizations from stable hierarchies to fluctuating networks and constant organizational transformation, and we have addressed it above. Whether this trend is in fact as pervasive as it would sometimes appear is debatable, however. In our examination of the context of loneliness in working life we will simply note that more flexible organizations can make it more difficult to achieve a secure sense of belonging. Both literally and metaphorically, it is difficult to find a chair and a place in today's less-stable organizations, and that may promote the sense of loneliness.

Working life may resemble one of three different kinds of parties: one where we arrive and find the place at the dinner table that the hosts have assigned us. The persons we are seated with may be boring or surprisingly pleasant, but one thing is certain: we have an assigned seat, which no one is going to challenge, and we just have to make the most of the dinner partners we wind up with. Other parties let the guests choose their own seating. That creates the possibility of finding an exciting group to spend the evening with – typically the people we already know – but it also contains the challenge that we have to spot and pick a seat, perhaps a seat that someone had intended for someone else. If we are bored, we have to make our excuses and find a different seat. The reception marks a third option, where everyone is constantly moving around, often drifting away when the conversation is about to move past polite small talk. It is nice to be able to move away from someone who drones on and on about perceived grievances instead of being stuck with them for an entire afternoon. It is tough to be stuck in a corner, hoping that someone is going to come over and strike up a conversation. The wine goes warm in the glass, and the hand grasping the stem clammy, as one stands there, hoping.

Being lonely is hard. It may be accompanied by a feeling of shame over not being loved or lovable. Loneliness seems to be perceived as an infectious disease that makes others keep their distance, out of fear that it might spread.

Psychological concepts for understanding loneliness

Loneliness and being alone

Being alone is part of the human condition. The capacity to be alone develops from the first days of life and throughout the lifespan. Being alone in a psychological sense not only refers to physical solitude; it also includes the psychological capacity to be *alone with oneself*. In psychology, the capacity to be alone is regarded as part of the emotionally mature personality. That is not merely about being able to handle or overcome being alone, with no one around or within reach, but rather being able to be oneself and to be in oneself. It is a fundamentally positive capacity that develops throughout life from the important basis that is formed during the first years of life. In *The capacity to be alone* Winnicott examines and describes this necessary capacity. He regards it as a sign of psychological maturity to be capable of being alone, without panicking and reaching out to others or busying oneself with distracting activities (Winnicott, 1958). We might consider the role of the smartphone, email and social media in this situation. Winnicott also argues that even though the capacity to be alone is sophisticated, in the sense that it is a capacity that is not fully developed until adulthood, it is based on the infant's early experiences of being alone in another's presence, primarily through the mother's or another primary caregiver's presence and accessibility – physical as well as psychological (ibid.).

Human beings are social beings who psychologically come into being through interactions with others. From a developmental psychological perspective, the interactions between the newborn infant and its caregivers are fundamental and crucial for psychological development (see, e.g., Eriksson, 1968; Winnicott, 1986; Stern, 1985). Winnicott says it very precisely: 'There is no such thing as a baby ... if you set out to describe a baby, you will find you are describing a baby and someone' (Winnicott, 1964), underscoring the role of the mother–infant dyad as the fundamental building block of human development. As one of the key conditions for the child's ability to develop into a well-functioning adult, the child has to experience itself as an independent and coherent entity, distinct from the world and thus a 'self.' A 'self' that is capable of development and change. However, being oneself is not the same as being lonely; in fact, it is a condition for *not* being lonely.

English distinguishes between 'solitude' and 'loneliness.' Solitude implies the ability to enjoy one's own company, to spend time meaningfully on one's own and to be in good company while alone. Loneliness implies being cut off from others, feeling isolated and unable to establish a desired contact with others. In the present book, we draw a similar distinction between 'being alone' and 'loneliness.' Being alone is an opportunity to be alone while still feeling appreciated as the person one is and being able to find joy or peace in one's own company. Loneliness, by contrast, implies an unwanted lack of contact with others. Loneliness implies an experience that important aspects of one's identity go unappreciated or even unnoticed, an experience of isolation, perhaps even cut off from one's own company. We may experience both loneliness and being alone in others' company.

We may feel both alone and lonely in the modern open-plan office, even when others are present. The seemingly open office space with no walls, doors and private spaces is not in fact open or without boundaries. The boundaries are simply harder to see and decode. The less explicit demarcation of individual territories and boundaries to meet on (and not only be separated by) makes our inner ability to draw boundaries and to express and represent ourselves important. It can feel particularly lonely to be without interpersonal contact in a room full of people who are in mutual contact. It may be especially important to be able to enter into dialogue with oneself when input from the external world turns to cacophony. In Elsass's book *Kunsten at være alene* he describes and examines the good form of loneliness, what we call the capacity for being alone. He describes how spiritual seekers need their mentors as inner figures they can relate to during retreats where they spend long periods alone. He tells the story of a Buddhist nun who, after spending 12 years alone in a cave allegedly said, 'I was never bored. On the contrary, there were days when I was surrounded by my mentors and aides, so that I could hardly get a word in edgeways' (Elsass, 2016, p. 104; our translation).

We can be lonely in a crowd, and we can be alone yet still feel closely connected to others. Growing up, the child has opportunities to develop their capacity for being alone by managing the sense of loneliness that are part of the experience. Loneliness may be partial: the primary caregivers may be unable to accept, contain or handle some of the child's emotions and instead deny and ignore them. Or it may be monumental: being all alone in a void. A good – or, with reference to Winnicott, good-enough – childhood will promote the development of the child's and, later, the adult's capacity for being alone. The capacity to be alone develops in the child's interactions with the mother as a capacity to be alone in her presence. Thus, the child's experiences of being on the outside, full of incomprehensible emotions, are either seen and contained or left to the child to deal with. Bion's concept of 'nameless dread,' which refers to the child's experience of being on its own and thus to the void, illustrates how overwhelming an experience it can be for a child to be left to themselves or to adults who fail to provide adequate responses to the child. Bion writes,

Normal development follows if the relationship between infant and breast permits the infant to project a feeling, say, that it is dying, into the mother and to reintroject it after its sojourn in the breast has made it tolerable to the infant psyche. If the projection is not accepted by the mother the infant feels that its feeling that it is dying is stripped of such meaning as it has. It therefore reintrojects, not a fear of dying made tolerable, but a nameless dread.

(Bion, 1962, p. 308)

Whether being alone is perceived as being lonely

Paradoxically, Winnicott explains, the capacity to be alone is developed, tested and practised when the individual is alone – with others. A well-developed capacity for being alone is no guarantee for avoiding loneliness, but the capacity to be lonely and to handle loneliness is bigger and better if the capacity for being alone is well developed. With a well-developed capacity for being alone, the experience of being alone is accompanied by the belief that it is possible to establish contact to others, or that it may be sufficient to be in contact with one's own internal objects. When being alone becomes loneliness, we no longer believe that relations with others is a possibility. We no longer see the point in reaching out or opening up to others, because no one is going to want to meet or to listen. Loneliness can be extensive and enduring and be perceived as destiny, a fact of life or a character trait, or loneliness may be perceived and experienced as something that is limited to certain situations.

No human being gets through life without experiencing situations where they feel alone with their points of view, interests, behaviour or experiences. Situations and periods of being alone can bring back earlier experiences of loneliness. Thus, both the current situation and our personal experiences with being alone and with loneliness shape our current experience of being lonely or alone. Psychoanalysis has shown, both in theory and in the practice of both psychotherapy and organizational psychology, how profoundly past experiences affect the way we perceive, understand and handle current situations. This should not be understood as determinism – that there is nothing to do, or that past experiences can be used as an excuse. Instead, it can enhance our understanding of the way in which experiences are stored in the conscious and unconscious parts of our personality and how they shape our future experiences.

It is unlikely that anyone will get through life without feeling lonely at times. In certain situations and contexts. The feeling of being excluded and wanting to be included. The feeling of being at the wrong party. Of having to holding back to keep from being rejected. The individual's particular experiences and personality make a difference. The specific internal objects that emerge and what they represent. Loneliness is not only a perceived state framed by our personal history. A person can be alone, unwanted or unloved, lonely. Or be completely alone with a certain point of view, a physical appearance, a gender, a difference that sets the person apart. That experience of being alone can be so overwhelming that it leads to loneliness.

Loneliness in organizations

Loneliness and being alone are not absolute concepts. Someone who generally has a well-developed capacity for being alone may feel lonely in an organizational context because they are alone in having problems or values that are not welcome in the given organizational context; as a result, if a difficult situation arises they may have to stand alone and act from that position. On the other hand, a person who is generally lonely in a given organizational context may be included in a community, which modifies that feeling. To that person, the joint tasks, shared responsibility and commitment to the organization that characterize working life may counteract a sense of loneliness that is otherwise a steady companion. Working life offers opportunities to develop and have new experiences – good and bad. It provides a context that may exacerbate or mitigate our sense of loneliness in open-plan offices, at the executive level, in break rooms, at conferences and in LEAN meetings, in everyday life or in particular situations.

Loneliness as family experience

The little boy sees his parents kissing. They seem to be enjoying each other. Immediately, he runs over and inserts himself between them. He wants to be picked up, included. The parents pick up the child; the kissing changes character, turns into more playful pecks on the cheek.

Feeling lonely in the family is an unavoidable and necessary experience. During the first years of life, loneliness may be translated into the capacity to be alone, but the child will also have experiences of being excluded from a relationship, feeling the nameless Bionic dread that is usually accompanied by the sweet relief of being rescued. The child is with its parents. But the child is also on the outside of their relationship. Having and surviving the experience of being excluded is a condition for developing empathy and curiosity about what is going on in and among others. The child does not know what is going on but is left to its imagination. The ability to wonder, with curiosity, about others' inner life and relations arises and develops within the significant relations of our early years. From birth, the child is part of a symbiosis, part of a trio, where they are outside the parents' relationship, and part of a family with (potentially) several siblings and with a past and a future. The child is not only part of a small trio but of a wide range of relations, past and future.

Feeling outside in the family is thus both a developmentally necessary and unavoidable experience and an opportunity to experience being the person who represents something unwanted or unknown. Who has personality features, interests or a sex that are not appreciated. Who is a little too slow, obstinate, precocious, ginger-haired, smart ... The list goes on, but many are probably familiar with the experience of containing something that the family does not appreciate. The question is what the cost is of holding something the others reject.

Inner self and outer self

The young woman pensively says to her mother, 'You all say that I'm so harsh, saying exactly what I'm thinking.' Her mother replies, in correspondence with her perception of the daughter's style, 'Yes, you're very blunt.' The daughter says, 'But I don't get it ... if only you knew the things I choose to keep to myself.'

We distinguish between intrapsychological processes, which unfold inside the individual, and interpsychological processes, which unfold in interpersonal interactions. Everyone has an inner psychological life. Thoughts, emotions, phantasies, sensations and other bodily perceptions. Dreams, fleeting impulses, worries. The experience of talking to oneself – in one's mind. Without thinking that we are 'hearing voices,' we sometimes talk to ourselves, both in everyday situations and in moments of heightened emotionality: what would be the right thing to do here? We may be plagued by doubt, desire may argue with reason, passion with fear. The various object representations may engage in heated dialogue or worried conversation, the inner mother representation from our teenage years debating risk aspects with the inner scoutmaster/guide, who argues that 'you are capable of more than you think!' Fragmented recollections of prohibitions and imperatives link up with our fear of making mistakes – associated with the voice of the inner aunt object: what would people think ... The generally well-functioning person is well aware that these are inner voices, no more, no less. Perceives him/herself as fairly coherent person with a body, an exterior and an inner life. This self-perception from within an as an inner self that may engage in self-dialogue while perceiving the external world constitutes what we call the inner self.

We connect with the world, express ourselves and receive impressions. The outer self is represented by speech, communication, gestures, movements, expressed emotions. The inner psychological reality and the outer psychological reality are connected but different. In order to conceptualize this distinction, we operate with the concepts of inner self and outer self. In Chapter 4 on theory we explain the underlying theoretical discussion of and development of these concepts, which spring from Winnicott's (1960) concepts of a true and a false self and Esther Bick's (1968) concept of 'second skin.'

The inner self thus constitutes the individual's perception and understanding of him/herself from within and contains conscious, preconscious and unconscious elements. The inner self is constantly evolving. The inner self may in part be verbalized and made the object of reflection, as outlined in the brief example above, but some parts of the inner self are beyond conscious reach: implicit, unprocessed or repressed. That may seem obvious, but it is important to remember that the unconscious is precisely that: unconscious; inaccessible to our immediate perception and reflection. Unconscious processes unfold continually within and between human beings and are unconsciously experienced. It can be difficult to give others an understanding of one's own inner life. In many ways, novels offer a way for us to understand both our own and others' inner life. The notion that others are distinct individuals comes with the possibility of discovering how they resemble or differ from oneself. Mirroring, recognition, wondering and shock. *So different, so similar.* What the experience is like when others try to understand – or change – one's inner self may contribute to one's sense of being out of place or unwelcome in the world or in the given context.

The outer self is the version of ourselves that we present to others. Part of that is quite deliberate, but we always communicate more than we are consciously aware of. Unconscious material is present in our communication, finds its way into our communication through our tone of voice, gestures, examples, stories. The outer self is both conscious and unconscious, just like the inner self. The outer self is thus both what we think and hope others see and what we show others unwittingly. Through language and bodily acts, such as movements and expressed emotions. The outer self is the basis of others' perceptions, interpretations and fantasies of our inner self. The outer self is both a defence, protecting the inner self, and a manifestation of our ideas about what it takes to be accepted, tolerated and lovable.

The inner self and the outer self are equally genuine and authentic. The inner self is just as original or true (cf. Winnicott, 1960) as the outer self. The outer self is our consciously and unconscious presentation of ourselves to others. It is a presentation that is only partially under our control. For example, the young woman in the vignette above is perceived as blunter than she intended to be, and she is a little surprised but not overwhelmed or shocked, as if she had caught a glimpse of herself in a mirror that showed her different aspects and angles than she normally sees in herself.

Let us look at another example: Jerry is nervous about a presentation he is going to give at a conference. He is well prepared, has written a script and worked hard on his PowerPoint slides. At the day of the event he puts on one of his nicest shirts and a suit. He does not know how formal the event is going to be, so he decides that if he feels overdressed, he can always take of his jacket. He considers wearing a tie but knows that he will only wind up tugging at it nervously and worry about whether it is straight once he gets into the swing of his presentation. The first few minutes of the presentation feel like an eternity. He sticks to the script and knows that he sounds a bit stiff. But then he makes eye contact with some of the people in the audience, who look as if they find his presentation interesting. He loosens up, speaks more freely, and without thinking about it consciously he says to himself, this is going all right. He allows himself to follow associations that come to him as he speaks, address others' questions and is happy to answer them. Most people in the audience see a man who took a little time to warm up but who did okay once he was past his initial awkwardness. Some might think that if he is such a slow starter he should not offer to speak; some recognize the situation from their own experience; some think that he should have at least worn a tie for this kind of event; others think that he is a handsome man; a few think of entirely unrelated things; and yet others think that the organizers should have invited them to give that presentation instead. Most of them notice the large patches of sweat under his armpits when he takes off his jacket, seeing a presenter who was visibly nervous but gradually got a grip on the situation. The perceptions of Jerry from within and from outside are not fundamentally at odds.

With Janet, the difference is more pronounced: she has slept poorly for some time. She has trouble keeping it together; she is not quite sure why she is having such a hard time, but she is. She has put effort into her make-up and dress and does not want her staff to see how badly she is doing. After three cups of strong coffee she feels that she is ready for the Monday staff meeting. At the meeting, the employees are highly critical of one of Janet's decisions. The decision is not particularly controversial or crucial to the organization, but it does lead to a change in the employees' daily work schedule, and they are not happy about that. Janet knows that the decision is necessary out of concern for the rest of the organization. She feels that she has explained her reasoning many times – too many times. When a staff members criticizes the decision again, Janet loses her temper and bursts out, 'Shut UP, mate, I have explained this so many times, you can't possibly expect me to do it again. Get with the programme, and face up to reality.' The employee tears up, the others look at Janet in shock as she walks out, teary-eyed herself. Janet sees the others as unnecessarily challenging, judgmental and critical of her leadership. She feels lonely. The employees see a blunt leader who indirectly threatens to fire a staff member and then leaves without apologizing or explaining herself. A few of them may have seen her tears and wondered what is going on with her. Some of them might have felt that the criticism of Janet's decision got too personal, but no one sees that Janet felt cornered, upset and lonely.

The outer self is appearance, representation and form, but none of those phenomena are independent of the inner self. It is an important quality to be able – or to try – to find the most appropriate way to appear in a given situation. That there is considerable variation in what different people perceive as appropriate is a key factor in interpersonal relations. Similarly, there will be great variation in what price the individual is willing to pay to be perceived as being 'appropriate.'

A person with a mature personality usually finds it fairly easy to assess and try to manage how they present the inner self via the outer self. What should be said, and what one should attempt to hold back. Everyone know the experience of being alone or lonely in a context or situation. Being the only non-believer in a group where everyone else is deeply committed to their faith can feel very lonely. To be the only person at a party who has never done line-dancing may be slightly less isolating but might still promote a feeling of being different and lonely in the situation, even though it does not rise to the level of a real problem.

The feeling of being different, that there is no room for expressing the inner self in the outer self is more problematic. It means having to deny inner self. In the example above, Janet does not consider it a possibility to share her frustration over having to explain the situation and her lack of alternative options over and over again. The specific incident may trigger emotions related to a more general experience of being alone in making demands and being fed up with that position.

The outer self is about behaviour and appearance, including clothing. The way we dress is not just about staying warm and protected from the elements; it also signals status, personality, gender and our perception of the situation. Showing up in a tuxedo when everyone else is wearing shorts or sweatpants is just as awkward as it is to wear a sweater and sneakers only to find up that everyone else is wearing a suit. Similarly, furniture and interior design also represent the individual's, the family's or the organization's desired and possible appearance.

Loneliness in working life

How difficult is it, for example, to dine alone in a restaurant? Does it feel natural, maybe a little boring, or is it just nice to be able to focus on the food, the view, the other diners, one's own inner life or a book? Or does it feel overwhelming, uncomfortable, as you worry that the others in the restaurant might think you do not have any friends, nervously fingering your phone or a magazine, finishing your meal quickly to get out of there in a hurry?

How does loneliness appear in working life? How does it present, how does it feel, and how can we understand it? In the following, we will look at loneliness from three angles: loneliness as a personal experience – being lonely with oneself; loneliness in working-life roles, with a special focus on the executive role; and loneliness as group dynamic. All the cases focus on specific aspects of loneliness but also serve to illustrate other points in this chapter. It is all connected.

Being lonely in one's own company

Feeling lonely in one's own company can stem from the experience of being out of place in one way or another. It may be a feeling of having thoughts and feelings that would result in shock or rejection if others learned about them. Finding that it is difficult or impossible to share thoughts, feelings or fantasies with others can exacerbate the notion that others find one's inner self shameful or wrong and even lead to self-blame for being that way. The sense of being wrong or out of place is exacerbated by an individualized view of success and failure, the downside of emotional capitalism.

Feeling lonely in one's own company can be understood as a discrepancy between one's inner and outer self, a discrepancy that is problematic because the inner self appears to contain unappealing, shameful or even loathsome elements. Elements that others cannot accept or which the lonely self struggles to accept. We call this *fear of exposure*, a concept that in our experience resonates with many who struggle with a vague sense of being out of place or being lonely without quite knowing why. Another aspect of feeling out of place stems from a sense of alienation. As if one contains incomprehensible, unappealing or strange qualities that are best left unnoticed. We call this concept *the changeling*.

Fear of exposure

Our interest in the fear of exposure springs mainly from practice experiences. We find that many deal with thoughts and feelings on their own, avoiding sharing them with others for fear that they would not or could not understand. We also find that to some people; these thoughts and feelings form an inner psychological reality that may have little connection with external reality. As if the individual imagines that they have something inside that has to be kept hidden or out of sight.

Gradually, we have also found that we call fear of exposure stems from a wide range of different sources. This means that there is also wide variation in issues and their severity and how simple or difficult it is to align with reality and to face one's own imperfections, shortcomings and troubling experiences.

In his later, more developed understanding of anxiety, Freud operates with three categories of anxiety: real, neurotic and moral. He pointed out (Freud, 1933, 1964, p. 85) that the original fear or anxiety may turn into a pattern where the original link between danger and fear is lost, but where the fear continues into the present, manifested as fear of seemingly innocent or non-threatening situations (see also the section on anxiety in Chapter 4 on theory).

The realistic fear of exposure in its simplest form is the fear of being found wanting, which may be realistic for someone who is only partly qualified for their job, or who is about to take an exam and knows that certain parts of the curriculum seem a complete mystery. That fear can drive us to make an extra effort to improve our qualifications, to focus in the situation or to find creative work-arounds to overcome our shortcomings. Fear of exposure may also find less adaptive manifestations. Devaluing reasonable requirements, resorting to fraud and humbug, accusing others of being useless or filing a formal complaint over an 'unfair' external examiner are possible, albeit maladaptive defences against this type of realistic fear of exposure.

Fear of exposure may also spring from a fear of revealing urges, feelings and fantasies that we would feel ashamed to reveal. To be revealed as petty rather than magnanimous, to rejoice in others' failure – maybe secretly spreading the story of the failure, feeling like a ten-year-old who has been sent to the principal's office, accused of being a troublemaker, when one is in fact a competent office manager at a meeting with the board. These feelings may go deeper, and since the process is in part unconscious, one may even have the sense of going behind one's own back: 'Should I really acknowledge that this too is part of who I am?'

Anxiety can also be fuelled by a relentless super-ego. A feeling that whatever we accomplish, it is never enough. Never being able to be proud of ourselves and our accomplishments, either because we would immediately discover that the performance was nothing to be proud of: 'You got an A, when you could have had an A*?' Or 'An A in applied mathematics – why, anyone can do that!' Or the super-ego might whisper, 'But the others will be upset if you show off like that, you'd better keep a low profile.' Fear of exposure that is driven by the super-ego can also be based on a fantasy of – or experiences with – being punished for being competent and knowledgeable.

In both examples, the person has to handle a major discrepancy between the inner and the outer self. Worrying that someone, maybe by chance, or 'any day now,' is going to discover all the terrible stuff we hold inside or discover that there is nothing there of interest. Asking oneself, when are they going to discover that I'm not good enough? That my professional qualifications look much better on paper than in practice? When is my house of cards going to collapse? When am I accidentally going to reveal all the embarrassing feelings and fantasies I possess? That I am basically boring and not very smart, and that I'm greedy and jealous of my co-workers?

There can be many good reasons to worry about not being good enough and for keepings one's green-eyed jealousy to oneself. The fear of losing others' respect. The fear may be perceived as being balanced, as a signal to remain vigilant. Jealousy of a co-worker's abilities and insight may be a feeling that we ought to hide as best we can; a familiar self-assessment: 'Jealous again? Well, best keep that to yourself, that's not exactly your most charming quality; you'd better learn something you can excel at yourself, rather than being jealous of others.'

Michael

As usual, Michael was up long before his family stirred, preparing for the day ahead, checking emails, ironing shirts and finding time for a quick cup of coffee before he was on his way. He always left around 6.00am, in part to try to beat the morning traffic and in part to have a chance to get through the work that was lined up for him. He used to leave with a smile on his face, looking forward to all the things he was going to get through that day. Now he had to pull himself together, grit his teeth to get out the door.

His wife was in charge of the family's morning ritual; that suited them both fine, and as the years went by, the kids increasingly took care of themselves.

Michael had worked as a sales manager in the fashion industry for the past ten years. Following high school, he had had a few 'wild' years, travelling, living abroad with a mate and attempting to set up an online fabric shop. That had been fun and challenging, and they had closed the company before it went belly up. Subsequently, he had taken a degree in business administration, meeting his lovely wife at the business college. The degree combined with his past experience and, not least, his drive, had led, first, to a job in the fashion industry and, next, to a better-paying, more exciting and more demanding position as Nordic sales manager for a major brand, which he had held for the past four years. Here he was responsible for sales in the Nordic countries and had two younger assistants. In the sales organization he had several good colleagues, who were in charge of sales to other parts of the world. The corporate management team included a CEO, who was Michael's age, and a deputy director, who had been with the company for many years. The management team had an open, inviting style, and Michael and his colleagues were expected to take active part in strategy development. They did, and the work was demanding, engaging and meaningful. There was plenty for them to do. Competition was tough, there were expectations of expansion and shareholder dividends. Michael was respected by management, who regularly expressed their appreciation of his work, and many regularly expressed their recognition of his contribution, acknowledging that Michael's flair for the business in particular had helped the company secure new clients and achieve excellent results. Michael too felt that he had a fairly good nose for what was going on. Whose star was rising, and who and what were on their way out. He still had some contacts from his year as an entrepreneur, chaps he would meet with over a beer from time to time in Denmark, Stockholm or London. But he also felt that the recognition he received was a bit over the top. Sure, he worked hard, and he was savvy, but he often thought to himself that it was more luck than brains when he landed a new contract or secured a new client. In fact, he felt that most of his success was down to chance, intuition and luck. Michael had always perceived himself as fairly average with regard to talent, diligence and competence. Maybe slightly cheekier than most, but that was about it, he felt. Over the years, a recurring thought had been nagging him: when are they going to discover how limited my talent is? When are they going to find out that I am merely, at best, average and thoroughly un-amazing? When are they going to realize that it's all a charade? Over the years, he had swept these thoughts aside, but recently, they had become more insistent. The popped up more often and stuck in his mind for longer. He felt that this in itself was painful, almost shameful. Certainly not something he could ever imagine sharing with his colleagues.

Michael is respected and delivers good results. How can we understand his fear of exposure? From a sociological perspective, Michael may be a victim of what Willig describes as the U-turn of criticism. The criticism is directed inward, as we described earlier, becoming self-criticism, rather than being aimed at the external world, at social or organizational conditions (Willig, 2013). Instead of being critical of the cut-throat competition in the fashion industry or of the calls for growing dividends for shareholders Michael unconsciously directs the criticism toward himself, perceiving himself as inadequate. Maintaining the sociological perspective, this is perfectly supported by the concept of the 'competition state' (Pedersen, 2011) and 'emotional capitalism' (Illouz, 2007), where the individual, roughly put, is responsible for their own happiness. There are good and plausible sociological explanations as to why fear of exposure is thriving and becoming so widespread at the same time as it is turned inward, individualized and treated as a taboo.

Michael's problems are doubled: he is suffering, and on top of that, he suffers under the shame he feels because he does not know how to stop suffering. He does not perceive himself as a brave man who holds his own, despite challenges at work and what is perhaps a slightly complex psyche, and who actually is quite successful. He blames himself that he cannot simultaneously work hard, keep the company successful and be happy on a personal level.

Sociology and sociopsychology can help us understand collective changes through a critical analysis of the discourses that frame our lives. Help us realize how we turn criticism inward rather than outward and see that the therapeutic mindset is not only a part of the solution but also part of the problem. This helps us understand how fear of exposure has become such an urgent issue. However, we also need to turn to individual psychology to understand the individual differences. Why does Michael struggle with fear of exposure, why has this affliction not hit his wife, his boss chef or his colleague, who is the sales manager for the rest of Europe?

If Michael's fear of exposure was mainly based on a realistic assessment of his work situation it would be susceptible to feedback. Feedback would help Michael align his perceptions with reality and contribute to a nuanced experience and expression of his competences. Feedback helps us learn where we do well, where we can do better, and improves our ability to rate our own competences and work performances realistically. We learn from our mistakes and shortcomings and adapt to reality. Adapting to reality also means acknowledging, at some point, that whatever the talent, it is now too late to become a top-league football player, that one's intellectual capacity is not enough to make professor, and that even if one is studying business administration with a view to becoming a CEO, not everyone reaches that goal, probably including oneself. That is realistic fear and alignment with reality.

Anxiety is not in itself a problem. New situations make us worry that we might fall short. Learning something new, building a new organization, raising a family and changing to a new job all make us worry that we might not have what it takes. Anxiety in small doses is both inevitable and motivational, but excessive anxiety is paralysing and causes the individual to defend him/herself at any cost, for example by avoiding reality in order to avoid the anxiety. However, having too little fear or being completely fearless can lead to passivity. No reason to try anything new and no pressure from burning platforms, aspiring colleagues or unsolved problems calling for a (better) solution.

Fear of the super-ego

Fear of exposure may be related to a fundamental fear of not being good enough. The feeling may be actualized in a given situation or period of life, but the source and form of anxiety go back years. We still do not understand why Michael is maintaining his negative self-image, why he cannot simply let go and enjoy his fairly impressive accomplishments. If a person is struggling with this type of fear of exposure and receives positive feedback on their work, the feedback may simply confirm the fear rather than allaying it. 'The boss clearly has no idea how things really stand if she's giving me such glowing feedback.'

An additional element to promote our understanding of Michael and his fear of exposure is to understand fear of exposure as attributable to the super-ego. The super-ego contains the internalized authority figures' demands, assessments and evaluations, as they were initially experienced in interactions with parents and other significant adults during the early years of life. Although these inner demands and assessments may subsequently be modified by new and different experiences, we should understand that the super-ego's relentlessness and insistence is imbued with the power of the unconscious. The super-ego harbours the conscience, that is, judging and evaluation, and the ego-ideal, that is, what the individual strives to be (Freud, 1933, 1964, p. 81). The super-ego has no difficulty with contradictions, illogical connections or chaotic reasoning. The super-ego is a tough master for many, difficult to satisfy. Michael might have a 'brutal' super-ego (Gammelgård, 2017; our translation), a super-ego that puts the bar so high that it is impossible to clear. That any performance is necessarily lacking. The ego-ideal dreams of greatness and success, while his moral conscience keeps him from being satisfied with his achievements. This dynamic cannot be righted with appreciating conversations and feedback; at best, that may offer temporary relief, before the person's inner life throws up new, unattainable demands. Michael is incapable of dwelling on his successes.

It is the role of the ego to moderate the super-ego, but sometimes the ego is not up to the task. The ego is busy. On the one hand, the ego has to regulate the impulses of the id, which is about as simple as showing up sober for a teenage party and trying to explain why it is reasonable to turn down the music a little. On the other hand, the ego is also in charge of trying to assuage and satisfy the many authority figures who may well form an endless line of parental figures, teachers, police officers, doctors, judges, kings and queen of Farawayistan who make forceful demands of all sorts of performances, better and higher, left and right. Endless demands are truly endless. The super-ego speaks with a forked tongue. It may be perceived as an inner voice imposing impossible demands: unhappy with Michael's position, he could have made

CEO after all. Had he become CEO, he could have made CEO of a bigger company or a company with better and more ethically meaningful products. He could have made more money, and still, the super-ego might point out that his pay cheques are ridiculously over the top. He could be a better man, stop looking at the young girls in bicycle shorts, he could stop being so boring and find a livelier wife, his children could be doing better in school and so forth.

Michael would probably easily recognize some of these claims as inner voices; the scale and the endless demands are so exhausting. Due to the contradictory nature of the demands of the super-ego he can never win the duel. There are other parts of the super-ego that he is less aware of, but that does not mean it cannot produce fear. Fear of a loss of love if he fails. Rejection, isolation, exclusion if he does not live up to expectations. The fear of exclusion and loneliness may be part of the reason for his perceived loneliness. Michael may be worried about exclusion and isolation. Perhaps he is occasionally overwhelmed primarily by nameless dread whenever he gets into contact with the sensation of falling into the black hole of the unknown. No wonder he is anxious. No wonder he is avoiding the issue.

The loneliness of his position makes Michael vulnerable. We do not know anything about Michael's childhood, it may have been completely average, and yet he seems to have failed to develop the capacity to be alone without being lonely. One possible hypothesis is that Michael, for whatever reason, has failed to develop sufficiently good and reliable internal objects to create and maintain the necessary sense of security to balance his fear of not being competent enough without facing an excessive burden

Discrepancy between inner self and outer self

Michael's outer self only has a limited overlap with his inner self. He shows parts of himself, while other parts remain hidden. This reservation contributes to making his loneliness painful because his self-assessment is never reality-tested. We cannot know whether Michael would be seen and understood by the people around him. Maybe they do not want to know how Michael feels and how he perceives himself in working life. In all likelihood, however, it would be helpful for him to be able to present more of his inner self, perhaps in his marriage, perhaps too a supervisor or a colleague that he trusts. We do not know whether Michael would see this as a possibility, as his fear of exposure makes it hard for him even to entertain the notion of sharing his concerns.

A person's upbringing is not sufficient explanation of the loneliness that accompanies fear of exposure. Sociological explanations are also not sufficient for helping us to understand the person. Loneliness grows, becomes more severe and can feel painful if the discrepancy between the inner and the outer self is too big. If some of the material in the inner self is perceived as shameful, too private or perhaps embarrassing, the person remains unconnected to others and thus lonely. The super-ego's contradictory and impossible demands are unlikely to be modified by reality and the meeting with others. We think that if Michael found the courage to communicate with others he might be surprised to find that others recognized some of his feelings or experiences, and that might produce some cracks in his loneliness.

Here we have tried to understand Michael's fear of exposure from the perspective of individual psychology. In closing, we should note that we could also apply a group-dynamic perspective on the individually experienced fear of exposure: that challenges or problems that exist in the company are manifested by Michael. We address group-dynamic processes later in the present chapter.

The changeling – feeling different

Sometimes parents have a child they do not really understand or who contains character traits they do not appreciate. Billy Elliot in the eponymous film is a boy who wants to be a ballet dancer. He grows up in a mining community, where ballet is not part of the cultural code. Almost like a modern version of the Ugly Duckling, with the added optimistic twist that the father eventually accepts the boy's choice, and Billy goes on to be a star dancer. We use the 'changeling' concept to examine and attempt to understand an individual experience of not fitting in, a feeling that is often accompanied by loneliness. The changeling is the one who has a problem, the organization does not perceive a loss. It is not a scapegoat problem, where an organization or a group uses projective processes to get rid of unwanted or difficult emotions, qualities or motives. The changeling feels alone with some of its qualities, interests and personality features, feels alien or feels that something inside they are alien, different, unseen. It is the changeling's own loneliness we are interested in here.

In traditional folklore, a changeling is a child believed to have been secretly substituted by fairies or goblins for the parents' real child in infancy. European history has many examples of popular beliefs that trolls, demons or other supernatural beings might steal a human child and replace it with one of their own. According to the Danish encyclopaedia *Den Store Danske* the changeling is ugly, has a large head, which may be soft to the touch, and small, crossed eyes. A changeling does not grow bigger with age, and even though it is a ravenous omnivore, it never learns to walk and is only able to produce incoherent sounds. A family or a group may treat a family member or a group member as a changeling. The individual may also feel like a changeling in the family or group: an outsider, a misfit, coming from another world, different, incomprehensible or unwanted. Let us look at a case.

When Helen turned 45, she decided to see if it was possible to change course. She enjoyed her life, generally speaking, but she had been plagued by a sense of inner emptiness that had taken its toll on her, and at times she had felt very lonely. She had two children with a man she loved. The children were in their teens now, had their own lives, dated, had friends and hobbies and mostly needed a well-stocked fridge and a chauffeur late at night when the buses were not running. She enjoyed her working life. She had an academic degree in the humanities, and after a few years of temporary project assignments and part-time work she was now in management, which suited her well. She headed a 5–6-person team in a cultural administration in a large municipality and had many interesting work tasks despite the constant budget cuts that, sure as rain, always affected the cultural sector. Nevertheless, she had an inexplicable feeling of emptiness that sometimes made her very sad and sometimes sent her on long walks, preferably along the water and ideally where she had a view of the coast on the other side. Over the years, her husband had grown accustomed to the way she occasionally 'pulled the plug,' as he put it. When she did, he waited patiently until she was back, asked no questions, was accepting, kind and supportive. So, she really had no complaints, apart from the gnawing sense of loneliness that often stayed with her after one of these long walks. When she was made team leader in her mid 30s, she had initially felt a great sense of relief over the added latitude it gave her. She could escape the collegial uniformity and do and think as she pleased. However, when she turned 45, the loneliness was so burdensome that she decided to try to gain more insight. She went into therapy, which made her aware of many things that she had not seen before.

She had grown up in a loving, down-to-earth family. Her parents had a small nursery, and her two siblings had chosen similar careers, one as a landscape architect, the other as a cook. She recalled a clear – and important, she now saw – memory from her confirmation. The main item on her wish list had been poetry. Danish collections of poems, collections of poems from other countries; she was especially interested in poetry from the Middle East. The parents had laughed kindly and given her a friendship book with blank pages where her friends could write a verse. The album even came with a lock and key. It was the kind of thing a 7-year-old girl wants, not a 14-year-old. From then on, she had kept a low profile and spent much time at the local library, where she delighted in reading the most enigmatic texts and, with less delight, felt very different from her family. She had followed through on this passion when she chose a degree in the humanities. Her study years had been interesting, but she had failed to meet a soulmate.

Helen gradually realized that her interest in poetry, especially from other cultures, represented a bridge to a seeking, dreamy, complex part of her self. She also understood that what made her sad was not her parents' lack of interest in literature and poetry. They had always taken an interest in all their children and had shown great commitment and dedication to understanding them. But they were unable to grasp what the poems meant to her. Gradually she noticed some of the same dynamics in her working life. She felt appreciated and accepted by the team members, fellow managers and supervisors. Still, she did not feel that they fully understood her, as if her deeper sides would always set her apart from others. Recently she had stumbled on an announcement of a literature conference in Cairo, a really niche event. Her supervisor had insisted that it made more sense for her to attend an advanced project management course, particularly in light of the upcoming renovation of the municipal culture and concert hall. She saw the point, but she still felt that the real excitement was going to be in Cairo, and that once again, she was not being seen.

This gradually growing awareness and understanding of a pattern that existed in both her working life and her private life was a relief for her. It alleviated her feeling of emptiness, which gradually faded. However, her feeling of loneliness did not go away. However, spotting and understanding her life patterns did gradually help her contain and handle her sense of loneliness. She was happier, but above all, she felt she knew herself better.

By our definition, Helen is a changeling. She has certain sides that she feels all alone with, and which create a sense of emptiness inside her before she understands what is happening. Helen has a good and well-functioning life and grew up in a loving and well-functioning family. But something inside her is not seen, is not mirrored; there is something inside her she cannot share with anyone. There is nothing unique or particularly unusual about Helen's story. Most of us sporadically, from time to time or in a more fundamental and general way have sides that we cannot share with others. The loneliness we are trying to capture here is the individual's own perceived loneliness. The loneliness that is experienced by people with well-functioning lives who feel that they have sides that are not seen or understood. Not because they are not loved or accepted, but because something inside them has or had poor conditions for being understood; as was the case with Helen's loving and down-to-earth parents, who somehow had a daughter with a penchant for mystic poetry.

The changeling, however, is not inherently alien to him/herself. We saw how Helen's sense of emptiness decreased once she began to embrace herself and her passion for poetry. The changeling has a clear self-perception that also includes standing out, being an outsider. Sometimes the changeling may doubt him/herself – am I simply wrong? Am I the only one who thinks it's okay to be a software programmer among literature graduates, a sceptic among believers or shy among extroverts? Or is there something wrong with me? Something I don't get? The changeling has self-insight but also feels left out, lonely in a group, without quite understanding the reason for this loneliness.

Michael may be lonely because his super-ego is strict and brutal. Helen's super-ego is not strict or judgmental. Her feeling of loneliness is more vague, there is nothing particular for her to pin it on, no specific fear of failure, like the fear that Michael struggles with. Rather, she is struck by the experience that there are parts of her self that are not seen and acknowledged. She is acknowledged, but only for certain aspects of who she is. She is alone with the part that is brought out and takes form through her interest in poetry, but which is about something other and more than poetry.

The changeling is not the one who carries the others' projections. That is what the scapegoat does. The changeling is someone who considers him/herself a stranger, someone who possesses qualities that others do not see or understand. In a sense, some aspects of the changeling are non-existent. One must not underestimate how difficult it can be felt when something is non-existent in the sense that it is not seen and perceived by others. With the concept of perceptive identification, which we introduced in the chapter on love, we would say that the changeling's experiences are that only what is recognizable exists, and what is recognizable is the projective and the projectively identified. From this description and examination of loneliness as an individual matter, we now turn to loneliness in working life.

Role-related loneliness

There are various types of roles in working life, and some are particularly likely to generate loneliness. For some team roles, group belonging is crucial, while others inherently involve being alone. Examples include specialists, freelancers, one-person business owners and, obviously, leaders. Our first focus in this section is on the leader – alone and possibly lonely.

The leader's loneliness

Leadership can be understood as a role and a process that takes place on the boundary of the group (Heinskou & Visholm, 2004; Bonnerup & Hasselager, 2008; Obholzer & Roberts, 1994). The leader is neither in (part of the group) nor out (outside the group) but operates on the edge. Regulating the boundaries between the group and the external world (task boundaries, resource issues, identity and other issues) is a basic and central part of the leadership task. The leader is part of the group but has a special role and task, they are at the boundary of the group, seeking to ensure that the group's dynamic processes contribute to the work tasks. At the same time, the leader is also part of the management system, a member of the management or executive team; with another specific role. Finding the right balance between being a member of the group, but a member with a special role, while also being a loyal part of the management or executive system, without losing touch with oneself or the team is a continuous effort for most leaders, and one that can be quite taxing, especially during the first years.

The capacity to be alone is a condition for performing the leadership task. To be able to stand apart from others and from the organization, without feeling cut off. Being able to handle being at a distance, reflecting, expressing oneself with clarity and making decisions. To be able to tolerate being alone in handling responsibilities and decisions – often and ideally in cooperation and dialogue with others, yet essentially alone. To have relationships with others that are enriching and supportive and provide input for the decision-making while also being able to act alone. To share and make decisions with the relevant persons, in the relevant roles, not with the persons it feels most gratifying to engage with. Successful leadership requires the ability to be alone. For some leaders, during some periods or in some constellations, being alone turns to loneliness. That experience is typically framed and, to some extent, co-produced by the special position and task the leader handles in the organization, knowledge that the leader is almost always alone in having and the specific relations around the leader in the specific context.

Sometimes the leader's role-based solitude turns to loneliness. Loneliness may be particularly likely to develop in a leader who is stationed abroad, where they are often factually alone, not only due to the role but also culturally and in terms of identity. However, loneliness may also develop in a leader who is surrounded by people they know and feels attached to. The following case concerns a leader stationed abroad.

Lonely in the company of others

Hank was tired. Tired. Tired. He had worked in the company for 22 years. Five years ago, he had been asked to set up and develop the company's Asian branch. He liked the idea of starting something new. Building something from scratch rather than maintaining what others had begun. Putting some distance between himself and his failed marriage and teenage kids, who did not need him anymore. Maybe it had not been much of a choice either. It was his career, it was important for the company, it was a good answer to many of his problems. And, not least: it was something he had been asked to do.

He had gone here, initially with nothing more than what he could carry in a suitcase. His plan was to make a more permanent move once the plant was up and running. He still had furniture in storage in Denmark. When he arrived, the plant consisted of a big – giant – empty building. The equipment for the production was lined up next to the building. Not installed or anything. It would not fit through the doors anyway. On his first day, he took off his jacket, resigned himself to the knowledge that his trousers and shoes would never be the same again and organized the workers to make the doors wider and taller. On day two, he helped bring in the machine components, and then spent the following weeks assembling machinery, establishing the production line, hiring, firing and hiring again. To a high degree he hired workers who were friends or family members of the existing employees. Easy and straightforward. Although it made things difficult when he had to let someone go. Then the bad feelings lingered for weeks. Or all the other family members left too. Still, he had stuck to the practice. It was easier. It also meant a good retention rate. Entire families relied economically on the factory. It helped stabilize the situation. He deliberately offered a pay that was slightly above average. He knew that a higher pay somewhere else would lure his workers away. On the other hand, he could not raise the pay too much.

Labour cost was a big component in the cost structure, and the competition was fierce. There were parts of the world that had even lower labour costs, and which also offered sufficiently stable business conditions. Areas and countries where Hank would never want to live.

He had many workers. Few spoke English, except for a few leading staff members, including a local mid-level manager with ambitions of taking over Hank's job sometime in the future when Hank left. A little too likely to give Hank the answer he imagined Hank wanted to hear. Not the best assistant. Maybe his key employee was a secretary, Suunaa, who was great. Competent. Hard-working. She had a grasp of the big picture that Hank sometimes lacked. She was married to an expat in another company in the area. The three of them might have been friends, but Hank had not taken the initiative, and neither had they. In addition, there was a Dutch mid-level manager, who had lost some of his drive. Grown a little too fond of the standard of living that was available to expats. Not quite committed enough to really succeed. But he was stable, a good business partner. Sometimes he said things about the local employees that Hank would not even allow himself to think. Hank did not really know any of the other employees. He did not want to.

Sometimes Hank missed the early start-up days. When he was literally, physically involved in installing and arranging things. When he would drop with tiredness when he came home at night. Pick it up again in the morning, his muscles sore from yesterday's labour. Now he was mostly tired from his efforts to make the workers stay. Meeting with suppliers and clients. Flying between Denmark and Asia. Flying out to meet potential clients. Having business meetings, dressed in a suit and tie, in air-conditioned rooms and driving in air-conditioned cars to and from meeting rooms, airports, restaurants. He missed development. Change. He missed being a part of the head office. Part of the executive team. A chat in the hallway, people never too busy to brag of their golf scores, grandchildren, lap times. He had no naive memories of cosy executive meetings; his memories were more about rivalry, competition, silence, conflicts and, sometimes, shared feelings when top management made decisions everyone thought was downright stupid. Still, he missed it. Missed the informal tone, also with female colleagues. Being part of the team.

When he was at work, he always stood out. He was the boss. Unsure whether the employees simply agreed with him to get on his good side. Unsure what they said about him when he was not around. Sometimes they talked about him while he was present. The employees often forgot that he had picked up quite a bit of the local language. That he understood what it was they were snickering about. When they wondered aloud about a decision he had made. However, he had never been able to have a sincere discussion of anything at the management meetings. He had often invited dialogue. Asked for their opinion. Asked about their hobbies. Their children. Anything. He had ultimately accepted that was the local culture. That people did not want to be friends with the boss. That they did not want to show the boss that they were better at anything, not even leisure activities.

The executive team in Denmark was not much help. They had visited when the plant was finally up and running – after an excruciating six-month delay. Everyone knew that Hank had given it his all. That nothing had been as promised when he arrived. That he had made a giant effort. Still, the CEO's speech contained only one single message: that now the plant was finally, finally, up and running. That they hoped they would soon be able to make up for lost time. That the clients were waiting, and the bottom line was bleeding. It was one of those days when Hank was pleased most of his employees did not speak English. He had made eye contact with Suunaa during the speech. Her gaze was neutral. Still, Hank read Suunaa's face as saying, 'Jerk. We just saved your bacon. The company's bottom line. Lots of Danish and local jobs. And you talk to us about rolling up our sleeves and making up for lost time. As if we've been twiddling our thumbs here, wasting time.'

Hank had had a few drinks with the CEO and the chairman of the board after dinner. They patted him on the back and said that he looked tired. Maybe he was spending too many nights on the town? After a couple of drinks more, they had asked what he made of the local women. They looked kind of small. Hank had given them a tired smile, looking forward to their departure. Of course, he went back to Denmark from time to time. Combining business meetings with family visits for Christmas. Easter. The summer holidays. The children visited him in Asia, but did not really know what to do with their time in his flat. Spend most of their time watching TV and playing computer games. During the weekends they went to the beach, into the jungle, went river rafting. But they never really clicked. Hank wanted to try something new. And then again, not. Kept himself busy. Joined a local golf club. Made some friends there. Did not think too much about his life. His work kept him busy, there would always be problems to solve. Problems to be sorted out. Responsibilities that were his alone. He had about ten years left until retirement. They would pass soon enough.

In psychological terms, Hank is lonely. He is surrounded by people, he has a large network. But he is not mirrored in a collaboration the way he grew up and was used to. He misses familiar and reliable relations. To management back in Denmark he is out of sight, out of mind. They do not see his hard work and suffering, and they probably are not even trying. Hank keeps his experience of the situation to himself. The executives may not actually be that interested, or maybe they are interested but do not know what to do, so they choose to do nothing. It may be hard for them to understand how painful loneliness is, and that their interest might in itself be important.

The loneliness Hank is experiencing is taking its toll on his mental well-being. Because he does not really have anyone to exchange ideas with, he is left to himself. Perhaps left to his own fear of exposure, fantasies of not being good enough – or the opposite, overestimating his own importance and contribution, which puts him at risk of making rash decisions with consequences for himself and others. Maintaining a healthy attachment to reality is only possible if we are mirrored in relations with others.

By virtue of the leadership role and the authority it implies, the leader is an excellent projection figure. We have all had the experience of being attributed opinions we do not hold, intentions we do not recognize, actions that are perceived as far worse or more noble than intended or motives that have no basis in reality. For the leader, that will often be an everyday experience. If the projected material is too extreme or too far from the leader's self-perception it may contribute to loneliness. If the leader is unaccustomed to or has little experience with spotting and managing projective materials, it may also intensify the role-based sense of being alone and push it toward loneliness. Hank was primarily lonely because he did not have sufficient relations that he saw as being aligned with his own perception of reality.

How closely the leader's perception of the relationship between his/her own inner self and outer self matches reality depends on the leader's capacity for self-critical reflection and for reliable mirroring in interpersonal relationships. For example, the leader who is perceived as tough and with no understanding of the employees' needs, finds that this attributes intentions, motives and competences to her that she does not really possess. She may tire of having everything she says interpreted in a way that matches a perception of her as an uncaring slave driver. She may either identify with the image and act increasingly without empathy, or she may become so intent on disproving the projections that she becomes anti-aggressive and shies back from making unpleasant but necessary decisions. If she sees and recognizes the projections as projections, she may act more reflectively, seeking to convey, through her actions and demeanour, that she actually invests both nuance and empathy in her leadership role. She may attempt to determine what the needs or issues are that led to these projections; this may help her find ways to handle those needs or issues in her relationship with the employees. If the projective pressure is extreme, the leader will find it difficult to be seen as who she is, with her good intentions. To be able to spot and understand the projective pressure may be a help, but it is no guarantee for avoiding loneliness.

Idealization is also a prison. Idealization is not realistic. No one is perfect, and if each and every act is made to fit a narrative of perfection, the effect is one of unreality. The idealized person will invariably disappoint, and the punishment can be severe. The competent leader, who is generally successful, not only has to deal with their own disappointment but also with employees', managers', the CEOs and perhaps fellow leaders' sometimes unreasonable anger and disappointment over the failure to live up to the idealized expectations and prove to be a mere mortal, albeit a talented one. The audacity!

It is easier to remain alone in one's role without being lonely if others can handle the notion that the idealized person is a fallible human being. Maybe the employees think of their leader as a hero, but leadership is less lonely if they can also see – and tolerate – that they are something other and more. That the leader missteps sometimes, makes mistakes, misspeaks. Everyone – including leaders, specialists, musicians and the canteen chef – have their flaws, shortcomings and off-days. Occasionally, these imperfections will be revealed to the people around them. Mistakes are made, in the kitchen and in the boardroom. Not every new song is a hit with the audience, specialists are not experts on everything. Most people are aware of that; the question is whether it is accepted. By them and by the people around them.

The leader is obviously not without influence in this. The leader's self-presentation, their outer self, invites fantasies and projections. We cannot unambiguously determine what projections and fantasies are engendered by a business suit, for example. But it will definitely be a different set than if the leader shows up in a flannel shirt and hiking trousers with zip-off legs. In one organization, casual wear means a light blue short and no tie; in another it means shorts and sandals. In some organizations, the staff look as if they have slept in their clothes; in others, they look as if they use the lunch break to get a fresh shave and touch up the folds in their shirts with an iron. The outer self is a representation of the leader, but it is also a representation in a specific organizational context, which becomes the background others view the leader's outer self against. In international contexts, we Danes are generally notorious for our casual dress code, although it may not feel casual but simply appear that way in a given context.

Apart from one-person companies that are too small to need a board, almost all leaders are mid-level – they have other leaders above, below and at the same level as them. In bigger companies there is a board, in public-sector organizations a political leadership. Thus the (mid-level) leader is viewed and assessed from multiple perspectives. From above, from below, from the side and from within. Depending on the leader's own experiences with relations in these different directions, they may attribute and assign – and be attributed and assigned – different qualities and tasks. In psychological terms, the mid-level leader may be understood as a promoted sibling (Visholm, 2013). The promoted sibling may, as Visholm describes it, have been promoted from below, pushed forward by and from the larger group, or promoted from above, having been selected, picked, as the right person to advance. That triggers many different emotions, both in the promoted sibling him/herself and certainly also in the group of non-promoted siblings. That generates projections, which may contribute to the mid-level leader's loneliness. As a promoted sibling, the mid-level leader is neither part of the leadership group nor of the employee group. From the perspective of a family hierarchy they are alone. From the perspective of an organizational hierarchy, one may hope that they find new 'siblings' in the mid-level leadership group so that they will not have experience loneliness or feel quite so alone in the role.

Role-based loneliness has much to do with the leader's structural position on the boundary of the group or, as described above, with having a role that is positioned *in between* sub-systems. Role-based loneliness is fed by the normal projective processes that take place between people, where some roles are especially likely to attract projections. In the story about Hank we saw how his loneliness was fed by his structural position, far removed from the rest of the corporate leadership, and by the fact that he was alone with a large and complicated task. We also saw how his loneliness emerged from relations where his leadership colleagues did not relate to him in real terms, as the person he really was. Moreover, the many employees and mid-level leaders he worked with offered little opportunity for relations that allowed him to feel seen and understood. This was in part, but not exclusively, due to cultural and language differences. Being alone in his role turned to loneliness. However, Hank also made choices himself. He did not reach out to try to establish a friendship with his secretary or take other initiatives that might alleviate or dampen his loneliness. It might appear that the role-based loneliness in Hank's case linked up with a more existential form of loneliness. When being alone in the role turns to loneliness there is often a personal component at play. If we wish to understand how and when being alone in the role turns to loneliness we will have to include the individual's personal history.

The trio – loneliness as a third wheel

In the book's main chapter on love we addressed pairs in working life. We described that many see the loving working-life pair as a core element in a meaningful working life. Being a pair requires the establishment of a boundary around the pair, a boundary that excludes those who are not part of the pair. Here, we will examine how some of these pairs may be understood as trios with an excluded third person, who will naturally be at risk of feeling lonely. The concept of a 'third wheel' captures this specific dynamic, where one person is redundant, in the way.

Trios are difficult in many ways, there is a tendency for them to turn into a pair and a third, redundant person. The Turkish–Cypriot psychiatrist and psychoanalyst Vamik Volkan has written about how traumas can be deposited and passed on through generations (Volkan, 2013). Volkan's transgenerational focus on how traumas can be transferred across generations has inspired us to look at the intergenerational relationship in the workplace and the dynamics that might play out, not only between the organizational 'parents' and 'children,' but between three generations: 'grandparents,' 'parents' and 'children.' As we see it, the hand-over of leadership from one generation to the next is a good example of these organizational pairs with an excluded third person. We are curious about how organizational traumas, hopes, visions of the future and reality-oriented behaviour are deposited and distributed in and between generations. How are these elements distributed among the different generations in the trios? The following outlines tentative reflections on one form of trio dynamics in organizations.

Frank, Paul – and Ed

Frank is pleased with his own contributions to the company. From a fairly small architectural firm it had grown considerably during his time there. Frank was now in his late 40s and had been with the firm for 17 years. He had been involved from the start, had helped win some big competitions, had probably also had a hand in losing a few, had persisted and redoubled his efforts when the financial crisis hit, and the owner, the charismatic Paul seemed unsure how they were going to survive without serious staff cuts. It was a fun and demanding workplace, and Frank was thriving. It was obvious now that Paul was running out of steam. It was time to find a new operational manager, someone who could step in as director. Paul could become the chairman of the board, step down partially but keep his finger on the pulse and maintain his say in the company's decisions. Frank did not really see any other candidates for the job as director.

Over the past few months, Paul had become increasingly irritable. He was criticizing Frank's work, decisions, presentations, points of view. Openly and in front of others. Paul had also begun to speak in very warm and appreciative tones about Ed's work and good ideas. Frank agreed with Paul that Ed was talented, although, at only 31, also a little green. Moreover, Ed had recently become the father of twins, which took much of his focus away from work. 'It'll be all right,' was Paul's comment, when Frank pointed out Ed's lack of attendance, obvious lack of sleep and usually very casual attire. Paul shared his thoughts with Frank: 'Don't you think he'd make a good director? He's got lots of great ideas, and coupled with your experience, I think he could thrive and develop the organization.' Frank frowned. He did not want to see a rookie, who had not been involved in building the company, as director. Frank wanted to be director, and then Ed could come next, when he had grown up. When he was no longer wet behind the ears. Done with having to stay home to look after sick toddlers and showing up with baby food on his shirt.

The vignette tells us nothing about the professional qualifications that might also play a role. We set those aside here and focus on the generational drama. The old man is about to let go of the reins, and the mature man is ready to take over. The young man is probably going to accept if he is offered the job. He thinks he has a great deal to offer and will no doubt learn what he needs to learn. It might be a story about accepting that the young generation at some point pull ahead, so their mentors become their subordinates. That is undoubtedly also an element in this trio's dynamic. But is also a story about the old man who does not like the psychological role of the younger generations: pushing him out of his working life and into retirement, a work-related patricide. The old man knows what he gets if he chooses the mature man: a murder and a number of changes. With the young man at the helm, the old man instead has a vision of a future. A vision, because the young man is not, to the same degree, an offensive reminder of the passing of time, but rather a promise that the organization will continue to exist for many years to come. It may feel more promising to see the potential of grandchildren than to see one's own balding children take over and pushing the old man into his (work-related) grave. There is hardly anything the mature man can do that would justify the murder of the old man himself. By contrast, the young man can miraculously avoid the murder – leaving it up to the mature man – and instead he can represent the promise of a bright future and great visions.

The middle generation may get lonely. Their efforts and qualifications unappreciated, unnoticed. Competence, experience, reality, results left in the dust by someone who instead represents hope and future. As if the middle generation could not deliver that. The middle generation may get lonely in this generational role. Their qualifications and qualities taken for granted or devalued. This loneliness in Frank – and probably many other in the middle generation, who see themselves as ready to take the helm in some capacity or another – is associated with big questions related to the cycle of life: when something new emerges, something else disappears. For something new to grow, something has to die. That is both a simple truth and difficult to bear. It might be a better decision for the architectural firm if Paul let Frank take over than by handing it to the relatively inexperienced and overstretched father of toddlers. But that is too demanding for him emotionally. Sometimes there are more conflicts and difficulties between parents and children than between grandparents and grandchildren. The latter relationship allows for the free flow of dreams.

It should be pointed out that relations between the oldest and the youngest generation can take a host of different forms. The idealization of Ed that we see from Paul is just one of many possible forms. Other (workplace) families have a different dynamic. Idealization, homicidal urges and reality may be distributed differently within the trio.

It is lonely to be the one who is excluded from an important relationship. Frank observes how the other two (unconsciously and tacitly) agree that he, Frank, is redundant, and that they can pretend as if there is no generation in between, a generation that has done a good job. However, the drama may reach a different conclusion: it could also lead to a close relationship between Frank and Ed, where they agreed that it was time for Paul to go, collaborated in pushing him out and leaving him out of important decisions, discussion, knowledge. Or maybe Paul and Frank would work together to maintain the current structure, and even when Ed is 48 years old, he would still be seen as the promising youngest team member, who may one day prove his worth.

Loneliness as group dynamic

Being alone and loneliness are relational concepts. Actual present relations affect whether a period without the company of other people is perceived as being alone or as loneliness. However, previous experiences of being able to be alone in others' physical or imagined presence influence the way it is experienced to be without another people's presence. We carry our internal relations with us, and the quality, nuances and reality of our internal relations are repeated and developed in our present experiences. Buechler puts it in the following terms: 'I believe who we are with, when we are alone, tremendously affects the quality of the experience' and 'the quality of our internal object relationships determines what it's like to be alone with them' (Buechler, 2011, p. 15 and p. 16).

So far, we have sought primarily to capture and describe loneliness as a personal issue and as an experience related to a specific role or position in working life. Here we continue by examining how the loneliness experienced and perceived by the individual can be understood in light of the psychological processes in the group, as group dynamic. Previously, we described how themes and states that shape the life of the group can be expressed and represented by individuals, and we have described how groups can disguise themselves as individuals (Bonnerup & Hasselager, 2008). The notion of the group disguising itself as an individual means that thoughts, emotions and experiences the individual has and perceives as its own spring from the group's psychology and can only be understood and managed meaningfully when they are met with this understanding. The phenomenon that groups thus, via projective processes, select individuals to handle a task, carry a problem or express a particular attitude is well described in psychodynamic organizational psychology (see, e.g., Heinskou & Visholm, 2004, Obholzer & Roberts, 1994, Bonnerup & Hasselager, 2008).

Being different can be lonely. The psychologist among the lawyers, the pedagogue among the nurses, the teenager among the elderly. The environment may appear as tolerant and well-functioning and may be perceived as such by most people, but the pedagogue may be tired of always being the one who has to notice and handle certain processes or always having to justify their educational background. Or always being 'the pedagogue' – rather than Chris. It is not always fun to be 'the only one' in a workplace, and it can feel lonely to be an appreciated – but alien – part of the system. A kind of mascot. Individuals may feel that they are appreciated, but for qualities that they do not themselves appreciate, or maybe they appreciate them but do not consider them particularly important. The aforementioned pedagogue among the nurses, who sometimes thinks that she would like to be Chris rather than 'the pedagogue,' may find that the others openly appreciate her ability to deal with the nursing-home residents who have dementia, while she wishes they would also appreciate her ability to show leadership and make the organizational routines run smoothly.

At Food for Fridays, Ethan was probably not the only one who might feel lonely in the executive team. But in the present context, we are not interested in Ethan's capacity to be alone or in his present or former life as such.

Instead, our focus is that Ethan may well have felt a growing sense of loneliness, feeling alienated or wondering why he was feeling a host of emotions that he did not used to feel. For a long time, he was alone in his effort to develop the wine import into a profitable business area. The loneliness Ethan felt during that period could be seen as the group's attempt to get rid of something that it does not want to own: the fact that sales are struggling in some areas, and that the company has to realize that it is no easy matter to get a comfortable share of the Danish wine market. Accept that the company does not have a huge safety net, and that it will at some point – and going forward – need to get by on a less lucrative market compared to the way things were when Food for Fridays was founded. Food for Fridays has to compete, differentiate and navigate much more carefully than it needed to when they were front runners in an undeveloped market. That insight and the orientation toward market and reality is delegated to Ethan for some time, and that makes him lonely. No one else wants to own or express the same concern, for even though it would turn out that both Rita and Carl had similar concerns, it was never discussed as a common theme or a common problem.

We will look at different kinds of loneliness in groups, where loneliness may well be perceived as a personal issue but should also be understood as a group dynamic. How groups delegate certain tasks or roles to individuals, who may as a result feel very lonely. How loneliness in itself is also something that may unconsciously be delegated. We will look at idealization and devaluing and the scapegoat mechanism as classic processes in group dynamics, which also generate loneliness. And finally, we will look at how becoming invisible in the group is a special form of loneliness.

The good, the bad and ugly – and the one no one wants to play with

In a previous publication (Bonnerup & Hasselager, 2011) we have used the concept of delegation as a group-specific concept to describe the process where part of a group is assigned and takes on a task on behalf of the group.

Delegation can be a conscious process, where both the group and the delegate are aware of the content of the task. It may also partially conscious, in that both the group and the delegate are conscious of parts of the delegation task, while other parts are unconscious, and finally, delegation may be unconscious for both the group and the delegate (Bonnerup & Hasselager, 2011). Conscious delegation has to do with tasks, competences and resources. For example, in a medical practice shared by a group of general practitioners, one of the doctors is typically in charge of examining a specific category of symptoms. That makes sense, given this particular doctor's expertise and experience. Delegation may also be partially unconscious: a task is delegated, but then something more is added. Perform this task, but do it in a way where no one feels dissatisfied, even though everyone knows the latter is an impossible demand. Our main interest here is with unconscious delegation, unconscious to those who delegates as well as to the delegate, because it has a particular potential for generating loneliness. The delegate is sent out to handle a task that is neither conscious nor clearly formulated. At one point the delegate may find him/herself trying to perform a task they have no idea was the one that had been assigned and accepted. Here, we will meet Steve, who had been sent abroad with a bigger set of task than he originally realized.

The delegate

Steve was enjoying the cold air in the office. At first, he had found it hard to get used to the shift between the heat outside and the cold climate-controlled air inside. Now he made sure to spend as little time outdoors as possible when he worked. His office was decorated in Scandinavian style. Simple and with Danish furniture, good, solid furniture classics and a photo of the wife and kids on his desk. He felt simultaneously mature and very young. A 60-year-old CEO would feel equally at home in the office. He had secretaries and a level of service he could never dream of back in Denmark. Worked long hours, but never had to shop, clean or help the children with their homework after work. They could just spend time together, go to the beach, play and relax. Much more than they would have been able to do back home. He also felt very young. Two years ago, he had been asked if he was interested in taking charge of the factory in Asia. Had been at a meeting, where the CEO had told the larger leadership team that the company's economic situation was not merely problematic in the long term, it was headed for complete collapse – in the short term. The solution was to send the entire production overseas. The product was simple enough that they should be able to train local workers. They had crunched the numbers. There was no other way.

Steve's first thought had been for the employees. They were going to lose their jobs. The company was in a rural location. Tough place to find another job. There would be problems, strikes, turmoil, press coverage. The thought of his own job situation had briefly occurred to him too. Maybe they would have to relocate. Charlotte would have to find another job too. And the children, who had just settled into preschool and school. When the meeting was over, the CEO and the HR director asked to stay behind. They asked him whether he would be interested in establishing the plant in Asia. He had the right age. Not too young, not too old. A family man. Responsible and dedicated.

After talking it over with Charlotte for a few days, he accepted. The CEO looked at him with pride. 'I knew that you're our man,' he said. 'I know you can do it.' Then he had negotiated a fairly good salary. Three months later he was the director of the Asian enterprise. A hundred local workers had to be trained, mid-level managers had to be hired. That proved to be the least problematic part. Steve was surprised that the cooperation with Denmark was the most challenging aspect.

At first, things were busy, but good. Steve had a mid-level manager with him from Denmark. Fairly young and without management experience, but committed. In cooperation with the three new Asian mid-level managers they worked out the basics. Hired the first 100 workers. Trained the first core production staff. Bought machinery, tables, chairs. Steve was busy, but he felt he could handle it. He managed to solve the many problems that arose along the way. In many cases he was alone in finding the solution, but the mid-level management team did a good job in executing his plan once he explained them what it would take. They did not really show any initiative, seemed to be worried what he would think of their ideas, but loyally carried out the decisions he made. He tried to teach them to be critical. Teach them that he needed their input. They looked at him, puzzled. Then gave him the criticism they assumed he wanted to hear. In a way, it was nice to be in charge. Without needing to debate everything. After a year, the Asian plant took over the entire production for the company. After another six months, the results began to show on the bottom line. The company survived, in fact it thrived. Steve was a success. He began to relax a little. Take the weekends off. Charlotte and the children were happy to see more of him.

Steve went to Denmark regularly. He knew that he was a success. Had delivered good results and solved major problems. He had a big responsibility in Asia and was well respected for his leadership and his approach to problem-solving. The only problem was that when he took part in leadership meetings in Denmark he was still treated as a promising mid-level manager, not as an equal member of the executive team. Certainly not as the man who had successfully guided the company through an existential threat. At the management meetings, new products and new production lines were discussed, and often, important decisions were made before he was involved. Although he was the one who would be charged with implementing them. To some extent, Steve could understand why the staff representatives in Denmark did not trust him. The probably saw him as the person who had demonstrated that it was not only necessary but possible to move production to the other side of the world and make other workers take the work just as seriously as the Danish workers had done. That it was possible to establish a plant with a high-quality output, where the much-debated cultural differences might have been part of the challenge, but not nearly as daunting as he been led to believe. There were disagreements and misunderstandings, mistakes, sure. But they were resolved, and he had no doubt that he was respected for his competence and skills. In Asia, that is. Not in Denmark.

The new production line was decided. The company was to put newly designed and developed products into production. There were some problems, however. The current machines was not up to the task, so the new line would require investments into new equipment and into training the workers. That would take time and would also require them either to reduce productivity in other parts of the company or hire and train new workers. Also, a big investment. Steve tried to bring it up with the executive team and in a meeting with the chairman of the board. He tried Skype meetings and memos, and although he was not turned down, he was largely ignored. At first, he wondered what was going on. Why was the interest so limited since everything really depended on what his factory could deliver? Gradually, his frustration grew. Why was he unable to get through to the executives? Was there something wrong with his leadership style? He was merely considering buying machinery. Hiring on a grand scale. Making all these decisions on his own. The chairman of the board had rung him a few days ago. In the middle of the night, oddly enough. As if the chairman had not thought about the time difference. Or could not be bothered. He had received a reprimand. Just because he had built up the Asian plant he should not think that he was home and dry. He was still young and untested. He should not forget his place. Carry out the decisions he had been asked to carry out. Stop constantly challenging the Danish executives. Put his house in order. Get started. Steve felt as he was a 12-year-old boy again, being scolded in the principal's office. He sat down at his desk. The cold from the A/C unit crept through his jacket. He had recently been contacted by another company. Would he be interested in taking over as director of their plant? The pay was good. And Charlotte and the children were thriving in the country.

Steve has been tasked with taking charge of a production that is being sent overseas from Denmark. Production is removed from its usual location. That creates unemployment where there used to be jobs and creates new jobs in another country. It is necessary for the company's chance of survival. That is the core of the formal task that is delegated to Steve. He has also been tasked, it gradually turns out, to do it with a minimum of hassle and cost. He is explicitly told that there is still a hierarchy to be upheld in the relationship between the Danish company and the Asian production plant.

The delegation of the formal task is accompanied by the delegation of a psychological task. On a rational level, a production task is delegated to a new Asian branch to secure the company's survival. In excellent fashion, Steve managed to get the production up and running and generate the necessary profit margin. Maybe helped along by the economic boom and maybe by a new design that makes the product attractive to new buyers. However, for the Danish executive team, this is not only an 'out of sight, out of mind' issue, as we saw in the earlier story about Hank. What we see here is a destructive devaluation of the accomplishment it was to build a new production in a foreign country. To understand this, we have been left to guess at the tasks that have been unconsciously delegated to Steve.

Closing down the production and cutting jobs in Denmark were a necessary destructive act to ensure the company's survival. The loss of jobs in a rural region of Denmark led to negative comments and criticism in the media. We might therefore wonder if perhaps the – necessary destructive – act was also supposed to be shipped overseas, whether it somehow became too much to bear for the current leadership. We might also imagine that the leadership's dependence on a fairly young man's skills and labour – and, not least, his success – has generated anger and frustration. Steve's success somehow becomes top management's failure, and his work and person must be devalued. The unconscious delegation of psychological tasks, processes and emotions generates loneliness. One is alone with something that does not really feel as oneself or as one's own. When it is difficult to connect meaningfully with colleagues, one is left to oneself. Steve did not appear to turn the pressure on himself in the form of self-criticism, self-doubts and self-recriminations. Instead, he appeared to be realistically disloyal in certain work relations where he did not in fact receive the acknowledgements he was due. Perhaps he will choose to switch to another company. Steve was sent out as 'the good' in the conscious delegation of rescuing the company. But he was also 'the ugly,' who had to personify the necessary destruction in Denmark. Perhaps this made him 'the bad' in the eyes of top management, the one who constantly reminded the rest of managers of the shared decisions. Hence, he had to stick to his place in the hierarchy from before he left, as the young, hopeful but inexperienced member of the organization who had to be kept at a distance. 'The good,' 'the bad' and 'the ugly' also became 'the unwanted,' the one no one wanted to play with.

Delegation occurs in all groups and does not necessarily lead to loneliness. Formal delegation is part of the normal distribution of tasks. Psychological delegation will always include aspects of unconscious processes. It is not necessarily a problem that one group member is in charge of optimism on behalf of the group, while another deals with reality testing and a third is responsible for novel ideas, as long as there is a certain degree of flexibility and reflection involves. It is always relevant to ask oneself what the source might be of one's own or others' perceived loneliness. The loneliness that springs from the group's projective processes can be hard to spot, however. Projective processes are unconscious, and there is a reason why they have remained unconscious. They contain something that is anxiety-provoking and unpleasant, something that someone wants to get rid of, and which someone is going to identify with. There can be many reasons why groups are unable to relate to or wish to get rid of the good, the bad and the ugly. Unconscious delegation is a way to understand and describe some of the projective processes that take place in groups. In the following we will look at two classic forms of projective processes that will be familiar to most people, and which may be associated with a high degree of loneliness.

The hero and the scapegoat

Idealization is a psychological process where the individual invests libido in another person (or idea or object) in an unrealistic way. Klein defines idealization as a defence mechanism that is closely related to its opposite, devaluation, and together idealization and devaluation are the basic elements of splitting: good and bad are separated, and one part is positioned outside the self. In groups and organizations, splitting is a commonplace process. In idealization power, competence, decisiveness, talent, skilfulness and so forth are attributed a single person via projection, for example the leader. An element closely related to idealization is devaluation, which is either placed into someone else, in the form of splitting, or takes the form of 'punishment' of the idealized person/idea/object for failing to live up to the unrealistic demands. Idealization thus turns to anger, disappointment and devaluation from others, who either replace their former projections with new ones – what an idiot our boss is – or who now have to take their projections back and accept their share of the responsibility for the aspects that were initially projected on the idealized person/idea/object.

Since the idealization has no basis in reality, disappointment is inevitable. Scapegoat dynamics, with their religious undertones, is a phenomenon where a larger group or society blame others (usually a person or a smaller group) for whatever it is that is not working, for example, economic problems, a poor working environment, uncertainty and confusion or other issues

Idealization, devaluation and scapegoat dynamics are widespread between nations, religions and population groups as processes that play out in the wake of global problems such as poverty, war, environmental problems and so forth, and we see the same processes play out in big and small context of working life. Idealization has the challenge that it appeals to the idealized person's narcissistic inclinations – who does not want to be seen as a welcome addition to the team, someone who can make a real difference, someone who is indispensable or the person that people are so, so happy to have as a director after living with bad management for a long time? A little intimidating, but also nice. It is tempting to be idealized, and maybe they have a point ... Idealization is often followed by scepticism. How long is it going to last, what might be next? This unease cannot be shared with the persons who are doing the idealizing; the idealized hero has to carry their elevated status alone, well aware that mistakes and flaws are not tolerated and will be punished harshly.

Idealization contains elements of mass psychology and identification. Idealization also confers an element of status to the group members through the glow of their own projection. Hence, demystification may be experienced as disclosure, disclosure of incompetencies or disclosure of everyone's narcissistic dreams. The idealized person is alone with their experience of having to live up to idealization and the sinking feeling that this is unlikely to prove possible. Since we are speaking of unconscious processes, which interact with other unconscious processes, they are both internally contradictory and difficult to discover and to align with reality. However, vague sensations of unease, of being seen as something other than one is, to play out and own feelings that are not genuine, are a sign that unconscious processes are at play and an occasion to reflect. What is *also* happening here and now?

At Food for Fridays, Vittorio is idealized in many ways. Initially as the Italian family's charming son, who had married a charming and beautiful Scandinavian blonde and created a lucrative business for himself and his family. For many years with the loyal and tangible support of mama and papa, who established connections, put in a good word, were proud of their son. The company underwent a critical period when it went into wine import and entered a highly competitive market that it was not really geared for. There was a period in the life of Food for Fridays, when it was not just Ethan who was worried about his ability to succeed, but when Vittorio also spent some long nights at the kitchen table in the company of his beloved espresso machine, which turned out countless cups of coffee to keep him and all his worries about the future company. He did not know what to do, other than making sure the company succeeded, trust Ethan, keep the management team together and, no matter what, avoid worrying Laura unnecessarily. Meanwhile, Laura was probably sleepless in bed, wondering what to do and worried about whatever was keeping Vittorio up. One afternoon, Vittorio had tried to make Fabio deal with the company's problems. Unaccustomed to speaking about worries, Vittorio was probably brief, and unaccustomed to hearing about his father's worries, Fabio probably was not paying enough attention. Following his general impulse, Fabio maintained that the situation could not possibly be *that* bad, and if it is, Vittorio can probably handle it, as he has done many times before. Fabio did consider, afterwards, whether he and Ethan could not weather the storm if it came to that. Even though he and Ethan sometimes got on each other's nerves, that was something they could sort out between them. If Vittorio's time was up, maybe this was when he, Fabio, ought to step in and take over.

Maybe that is the explanation for Vittorio's striking lack of interest in the article in *Manly*: that on the one hand, he felt very alone with the responsibility and the conscious and unconscious demands to solve the problems at any cost, and on the other hand, he saw his son being idealized in a magazine, idealized for something he had not built himself. Truth be told, Vittorio sometimes wondered about Fabio's work ethic, whether he would be able to work as hard as he, Vittorio, had worked, and as he would need to do in the future.

Being invisible in the group

So far, we have described how loneliness as a group dynamic can stem from projective processes, as the individual may, in various ways, feel alone with something that belongs in the group. To round off our study of loneliness as a group dynamic, we propose the opposite point: that loneliness can also occur when someone is very much 'in.' We are always part of several groups, whether we like it or not, whether we are physically together or not, and regardless what the groups' formal and informal tasks are. In any group it is a constant challenge to find the balance between adapting to the group and finding one's own position in the group or next to the group. In contrast to the delegation processes we will now look at a dynamic where the individual may have the experience of getting lost in the group and feeling lonely, because they are not allowed to have any unique personal features. Only the group's beliefs, norms, characteristics are allowed. That may be an internal group dynamic or it may be the result of the external world's perception of the group. Probably more than a few school teachers were fed up with having to represent and defend the profession when the Danish school reforms were implemented during the mid 2010s? Felt that in many contexts they disappeared as persons and were seen only as 'a school teacher'? That personal characteristics and independent points of view disappeared.

Clear group belonging can also lead to loneliness. When the individual's personal features and identity disappear, the members of the majority may paradoxically feel lonely. Precisely because they are not seen as individuals but as representatives of a group, their identity defined by their group membership, and their individual characteristics disappearing in the mass label. In his influential work with groups Bion has described this duality of groups. Individuals orient toward the group as a place where they can have their needs met and adapt to what Bio calls the *group mentality:* the group's unanimous will, which shapes thoughts and thinking and acts (Bion, 1968 pp. 50ff). The group can soothe anxiety by providing a containing function, where the individual is seen and contained with their peculiarities and unique features. The group may also generate anxiety because it is perceived as aggressive and invasive, and the individual may feel that the group challenges or attacks their individuality (ibid.).

Anyone may come to doubt their own judgment and grasp of reality, our ability to stand alone may be gradually eroded if our loneliness lasts a long time, if our environment is isolating, if it is difficult to maintain our ability to take a nuanced and explorative view of situations. Everyone has experiences with giving in to peer pressure, doubting their own opinions and values. Most people also have experience with doubting their own assessment of a situation – am I seeing this right? These earlier and perhaps painful situations may trigger and bring emotions or emotional qualities into the situation that are not related to the current situation but to a previous one. A current difficult situation may activate the emotions and experiences related to a previous situation. It is not easy to learn from experience; it sounds so constructive, but sometimes the lesson we learn from our experiences is destructive.

Closing remarks

It is difficult to imagine a life that does not involve the experience of loneliness. Being excluded is a basic experience, just as most people also, fortunately, have basic experiences of being included in a community. There are good sociological and sociopsychological explanations for the emergence and experience of loneliness and a basis for claiming that loneliness is inherently damaging to our health. Loneliness comes in many different variants in organizational and working life. Loneliness associated with the fear of exposure, associated with the experience of being out of place, associated with one's formal or informal role in the organization or loneliness as part of a group dynamic. From an individual psychological perspective, the capacity to be alone and the ego's ability to handle fear in a reality-oriented and dynamic manner are crucial for the way we experience, perceive and survive loneliness.

Working life is the setting for much of our life, and for many of us, it is an important part of the substance of our life and our identity. Unconscious processes may be destructive and exclusive, but they may also be creative and promote development. Part of the loneliness that exists in working life is produced in and by the roles and communities we enter into and contribute to.

References

Armstrong, D. (2005). Emotions in organisations. disturbance or intelligence? In D. Armstrong (2005). *Organization in the mind. Psychoanalysis, group relations and organizational consultancy.* London, UK: Karnac.

Armstrong, D., & Rustin, M. (2015). *Social defences against anxiety.* London, UK: Karnac.

Beck, U. (1992). *Risk society. Toward a new modernity.* London, UK: Sage.

Bick, E. (1968). The experience of skin. *International Journal of Psycho-analysis*, 49, 484–486.

Bion, W. (1962). The psycho-analytic study of thinking. *International Journal of Psycho-analysis*, 43, 306–310.

Bion, W. (1968). *Experiences in groups.* London, UK: Tavistock Publications.

Bonnerup, B., & Hasselager, A. (2008). *Gruppen på arbejde.* Copenhagen, Denmark: Hans Reitzels Forlag.

Bonnerup, B., & Hasselager, A. (2011). Ledelse af læreprocesser i grupper. In P. Helth (Ed.), *Ledelse og læring i praksis.* Copenhagen, Denmark: Forlaget Samfundslitteratur.

Brinkmann, S. (2011). Følelser på godt og ondt. In C. Elmholdt & L. Tanggaard (Eds.), *Følelser i ledelse.* Århus, Denmark: Klim.

Buechler, S. (2011). Someone to watch over me. In B. Willock (Ed.), *Loneliness and longing. Conscious and unconscious aspects.* London, UK: Routledge.

Damasio, A. (2012). *Self comes to mind.* New York, NY: Pantheon Books.

Elmholdt, C., & Tanggaard, L. (2011). *Følelser i ledelse.* Århus, Denmark: Klim.

Elsass, P. (2016). *Kunsten at være alene.* Copenhagen, Denmark: Gyldendal.

Eriksson, H. E. (1968). *Identitet, ungdom og kriser.* Copenhagen, Denmark: Hans Reitzel.

Fineman, S. (2003). *Understanding emotion at work.* London, UK: Sage.

Freud, A. (1993). *The ego and the mechanisms of defence.* London, UK: Karnac. (Original work published 1936.)

Freud, S. (1964). New introductory lectures on psycho-analysis and other works. In J. Strachey (Ed. and Trans.), *The standard edition of the complete psychological works of Sigmund Freud (Vol. 22)*. London, UK: Hogarth. (Original work published 1933.)

Gammelgård, J. (2017). *Om psykoanalyse*. Lecture at MPO, Roskilde University, 25 January.

Giddens, A. (1990). *The consequences of modernity*. Stanford, CA: Stanford University Press.

Giddens, A. (1991). *Modernity and self-identity*. Stanford, CA: Stanford University Press.

Heinskou, T., & Visholm, S. (2004). *Psykodynamisk organisationspsykologi. På arbejde under overfladen*. Copenhagen, Denmark: Hans Reitzels Forlag.

Illouz, E. (2007). *Cold intimacies. The making of emotional capitalism*. Cambridge, UK: Polity.

Illouz, E. (2012). *Why love hurts. A sociological explanation*. Cambridge, UK: Polity.

Jemsted, A. (2011). Introduction. In C. Bollas (Ed.), *The Christopher Bollas reader*. New York, NY: Routledge.

Karpatschof, B., & Katzenelson, B. (2011). *Klassisk og moderne psykologisk teori*. Copenhagen, Denmark: Hans Reitzels Forlag.

Klein, M. (1952). *The Writings of Melanie Klein, volume 8: Envy and gratitude and other works*. London, UK: Hogarth.

Lasgaard, M., & Friis, K. (2014). *Ensomhed blandt voksne*. Århus, Denmark: CFK – Folkesundhed og kvalitetsudvikling. Region Midtjylland.

Lasgaard, M., & Friis, K. (2015). *Ensomhed i befolkningen*. Århus, Denmark: CFK – Folkesundhed og kvalitetsudvikling. Region Midtjylland.

Miller, E. J., & Rice, K. A. (1975). Selections from: Systems of organizations. In A. D. Colman & H. Bexton (Eds.), *Group relations reader 1*. Washington, DC: A. K. Rice Institute.

Morgan, G. (2006). *Images of organization*. London, UK: Sage.

Nielsen, B. S., & NielsenE. (1978). *Socialisationsforskning*. Copenhagen, Denmark: Borgen Basis.

Obholzer, A., & Roberts, V. Z. (Eds.) (1994). *The unconscious at work*. London, UK/ New York, NY: Routledge.

Olsen, O. A. (Ed.) (2002). *Psykodynamisk leksikon*. Copenhagen, Denmark: Gyldendal.

Olsen, O. A., & Køppe, S. (1981). *Freuds psykoanalyse*. Copenhagen, Denmark: Gyldendal.

Pedersen, O. K. (2011). *Konkurrencestaten*. Copenhagen, Denmark: Hans Reitzels Forlag.

Pedersen, S. H. et al. (2010). Affektregulering – holding, containing og spejling. *Psyke & Logos*, 31, 552–576.

Petersen, E., & Sabroe, K. E. (1984). *Arbejdspsykologi*. Copenhagen, Denmark: Munksgård.

Rosa, H. (2010). *Alienation and acceleration*. Århus, Denmark: Aarhus University Press.

Scalia, J. (2002) (Ed.). *The vitality of objects*. London, UK: Continuum.

Scharmer, O. (2007). *Theory U: Leading from the future as it emerges*. Cambridge, MA: The Society for Organizational Learning.

Sennett, R. (1998). *The corrosion of character. The personal consequences of work in the new capitalism*. New York, NY: Norton.

Stern, D. (1985). *The interpersonal world of the infant*. New York, NY: Basic Books.
Visholm, S. (2013). *Forfremmede søskende. Om åben og skjult familiedynamik i organisationer*. Copenhagen, Denmark: Hans Reitzels Forlag.
Volkan, V. (2013). *Animal killer*. London, UK: Karnac Books.
Volpert, W. (1980). *Lønarbejdets psykologi*. Copenhagen, Denmark: Hans Reitzels Forlag.
Willig, R. (2013). *Kritikkens u-vending*. Copenhagen, Denmark: Hans Reitzels Forlag.
Willig, R. (2016). *Afvæbnet kritik*. Copenhagen, Denmark: Hans Reitzels Forlag.
Willock, B. et al. (2012). *Loneliness and longing*. London, UK: Routledge.
Winnicott, D. (1958). The capacity to be alone. *International Journal of Psycho-analysis*, 39(5), 416–420.
Winnicott, D. (1960). Ego distortion in terms of true and false self. In D. Winnicott (1965). *The maturational processes and the facilitating environment* (Chp 12). London, UK: Karnac.
Winnicott, D. (1964). Further thoughts on babies as persons. In D. Winnicott (1964). *The child, the family, and the outside world* (pp. 85–92). Harmondsworth, UK: Penguin. (Original work published 1947.)
Winnicott, D. (1971). *Playing and reality*. London, UK: Tavistock.
Winnicott, D. (1986). *Home is where we start from*. London, UK: Penguin.

Online sources

www.psykiatrifonden.dk
www.denstoredanske.dk, Den store danske encyklopædi.

Chapter 4

Theory

The unconscious – a key concept in psychoanalysis

Psychoanalysis was, of course, founded by Sigmund Freud, who formulated his ground-breaking theories from the late 19th century until his death in 1938. Contemporaneously with Freud and after his death, a host of new developments, reformulations and innovations have emerged. Psychoanalysis comprises a diversity of theories and can hardly be described in the singular (see, e.g., Zeuthen & Køppe, 2014). Our principal purpose in this first section is to present and debate the psychoanalytic concept of the unconscious. This is a courageous attempt. In a limited number of pages, we seek to capture this crucial aspect of psychoanalytic and psychodynamic theory, a concept that marks a definitive distinction between the dynamic theories and other psychological theories.

Models of the psychological apparatus

Freud formulated two topical models of the psychological apparatus. Both models combine, in different ways, with his theories of psychological development. The first topical model includes the elements the conscious, the preconscious and the unconscious and are formulated in Freud's *The interpretation of dreams* (first part and second part) (Freud, 1953a, 1953b), key treatises in Freud's work. The preconscious can be described as the guard between the conscious and the unconscious; the material here is not in itself conscious but may become so – or it may be repressed, relegated to the unconscious. Material from the unconscious may intrude, and in the preconscious it may be transformed into material that 'slips through' the censorship, for example in jokes, mistakes and so-called Freudian slips (Freud, 1905/1960).

In 1923 Freud introduced the second topical model, which consists of the ego, the super-ego and the id. The ego is a concept that Freud used throughout his authorship, although the meaning varied slightly over the years. The ego serves a central function in regulating the relationship with reality, and the ego contains the individual's self-concept. The ego is also the seat of our defence mechanisms, which are largely unconscious dynamic processes; thus, the ego also contains unconscious processes, just as both the id and the super-ego consists of unconscious processes. Freud writes about the ego in the article 'The ego and the id' from 1923:

> We see this same ego as a poor creature owing service to three masters and consequently menaced by three dangers: from the external world, from the libido of the id, and from the severity of the super-ego. Three kinds of anxiety correspond to these three dangers, since anxiety is the expression of a retreat from danger.
> (Freud, 1923/1961, pp. 1–66)

And in *Outline of psychoanalysis*, Freud's last treatise and published posthumously, he writes,

> the severest demand upon the ego is probably the keeping down of the instinctual claims of the id ... But the claims made by the super-ego, too, may become so powerful and so remorseless that the ego may be crippled, as it were, for its other tasks. We may suspect that ... the id and the super-ego often make common cause against the hard-pressed ego, which in order to retain its normal state, clings on to reality.
> (Freud, 1939/1964b, p. 62)

It is almost hard not to feel sorry for this hard-pressed ego. This is the model that some call the structural model, a term that Freud himself only used once (Køppe, 2002).

Object

Object is another key concept in psychoanalysis and also a concept with a complex meaning. Objects are both the real physical objects (persons, things) and the psychological representation of the object in our psyche, notions of the object or the object representation, as it also called. For example, the actual real mother is internalized into an inner representation of the mother in the child's psyche. Objects, too, are internalized, as components: breast, arms, bed, for example, which are internalized as partial objects. It is not only the breast, the arm and the bed that are internalized but the entire experience, 'I am enclosed by warmth, security, food,' that is internalized as an experiential form associated with the partial objects. In Melanie Klein's work the object concept occupies a central role, and object relations theory operates with good and bad objects, whole objects and partial objects and internal and external objects, all parts of our inner mental life (Klein, 1952).

The unconscious

Our aim here is to present the rich wealth of the concept of the unconscious, rather than to try to provide a complete answer to the question, 'what is the unconscious?' Like the unconscious itself, the concept of the unconscious contains endless contradictions, inspiration and nuance. Freud said in a lecture in 1932,

> The oldest and best meaning of the word 'unconscious' is the descriptive one; we call a psychical process unconscious whose existence we are obliged to assume – for some such reason as that we infer it from its effects –, but of which we know nothing. In that case we have the same relation to it as we have to a psychical process in another person, except that it is in fact one of our own.
>
> (Freud, 1933/1964a, p. 70)

And further:

> Its [therapy's] intention is, indeed, to strengthen the ego, to make it more independent of the super-ego, to widen its field of perception and enlarge its organization, so that it can appropriate fresh portions of the id. Where id was, there ego shall be. It is a work of culture – not unlike the draining of the Zuydersee.
>
> (ibid., p. 80)

The unconscious is a central concept in psychoanalytic thinking, at once very controversial and a concept that has become part of everyday language. The unconscious is both a potential insult and a wealth. An insult because it reminds us that 'the ego is not master in its own house' (Freud, 1917/1955a, p. 143). A wealth exactly because the unconscious is *not* limited by logical connections, consistency and adaptation to reality. Moreover, the unconscious also contains the drives and the libido and the capacity to think unthought thoughts (Bion, 1968; Bollas, 1987) and to create impossible combinations.

In fact, it was not Freud who introduced the concept of the unconscious, the concept was already current in the late 19th century (see, e.g., Thielst, 2006). Freud, as Olsen and Vedfelt describe it, gave the concept an 'acid bath,' cleansing it of simply containing all sorts of aspects we happened not to be consciously aware of (Olsen & Vedfelt, 2002). With Freud's more refined and precise definition, the concept became both highly debated and a construct that helped us understand and explain behaviour that had previously seemed incomprehensible. Freud's thinking was controversial in many regards, perhaps less due to his use of the concept of the unconscious and more due to his ideas about what the unconscious contains: the child's sexuality, the destructive and chaotic workings of the unconscious, penis envy, fear of castration, incestuous phantasies. The content of the unconscious was, and in many ways still remains today, difficult to understand and accept. The unconscious as a concept is a theoretical abstraction; can and sense its presence through its influence on our actions. 'The unconscious does not exist, but it insists,' as Rösing puts it (Rösing, 2007; our translation).

The unconscious contains a diverse range of material

First of all, the unconscious contains material that was unconscious from the outset, and which the ego confines to the unconscious. Drives and impulses that the ego knows should not be accessible. Not only is the material unconscious and kept in check by means of repression, the repression too is unconscious. This 'pre-repressed' material can find its way through the palisades of the defence mechanisms, through slips, displacements, missteps and so forth. The unconscious also contains material that was conscious but which has been repressed, just as the repression too may repressed. There is no processing of the repressed in the unconscious. 'There is nothing in the id that corresponds to the idea of time; there is no recognition of the passage of time and ... no alteration in its mental process is produced by the passage of time. Wishful impulses which have never passed beyond the id, but impressions, too, which have been sunk into the id by repression, are virtually immortal; after the passage of decades they behave as though they had just occurred' (Freud, 1933/1964a, p. 74).

The unconscious contains memories of traumatic events. This includes experiences that most would recognize as being traumatic, such as abuse, actual loss of love objects, threats or bodily harm and the transgression of personal boundaries. It also includes experiences that others do not recognize as being traumatic, but which in the child's imagination *become* traumas. They remain traumatic experiences in the child's and later the adult's life if they remain unconscious and unprocessed, precisely because they remain in the unconscious while constantly exercising a pressure on the ego and its defence mechanisms.

A third element for understanding the dynamics of the unconscious is the concept of 'afterwardsness' (from the German '*Nachträglichkeit*'). This concept 'not only refers to an earlier event only being understood at a later time. On the contrary, the earlier event only comes into existence as an impactful phenomenon at a later time and only then becomes traumatic' (Gammelgård, 2011, p. 167; our translation). An event at first appears innocent to the child, but as the child develops, and sometimes not until adulthood, and with the growing understanding that emerges, the event unfolds in retrospect, and it is only then that it is transmuted into a traumatic event. This could be the child's sexual play, or it could be interactions with adults that do not appear as abuse to the child in the situation, but which, upon recollection, are perceived and experienced as traumatizing with the growing awareness of personal boundaries and the boundaries between generations and sexes. Afterwardsness underscores that the psyche does not operate with a standard chronological cause-and-effect chain, and that 'the psyche is ... handed a task, a task that consists in a continuous translation of impression that have formed early in life – impressions from which we can only retroactively wrest their enigmatic meaning' (Zeuthen et al., 2008, p. 436; our translation).

Repetition compulsion

Repetition compulsion is a concept that may explain much seemingly meaningless behaviour or even repeated suffering. A pressure from the unconscious causes the individual to repeat situations and patterns by putting him/herself into situations where they experience a repetition of the traumatic events. The phenomenon may have several explanations. Repetition compulsion may be understood as a manifestation of the death drive – a self-destructive urge within the individual, either as a recurring return to the absence of tension between desire and the satisfaction of desire or as an actual drive toward destruction, the death drive (Freud, 1921/1955b).

Repetition compulsion may also be understood as repetition driven by a fear that the inner structure might collapse because, regardless how unpleasant a familiar pattern is when it is experienced and repeated, it is still familiar and predictable. The notion of an alternative may above all imply the notion of what Bion called nameless dread (Bion, 1962), the completely unimaginable, empty space. Repetition compulsion may also be experiential, where the experience or notion is that other states are even harder to handle. This notion may be more or less reality-based, and thus, it may primarily be unconscious phantasies of unimaginable terror that dominate, not actual experiences of unimaginable, nameless horrors. Importantly, however, experiences concerning treats of the loss of love, dignity or an intact body may be quite reality-based notions and experiences that are brought back by current experiences.

Repetition compulsion may also be understood as a desire for repair, a different outcome to a traumatic event, taking the active rather than the passive role. The person may seek out situations where the pattern repeats itself, but with the hope of gaining new experiences, being the active participant rather than someone who is passively subjected to someone else's actions (see more about passive–active polarity in Olsen and Køppe, 1981). Perhaps, the experience will be yet another painful repetition that may lead to further confirmation of the initial traumatic situation or of a maladaptive relational pattern. In a different sense, repetition compulsion may also be a manifestation of the particularly creative and intrusive form of the unconscious, repeating something over and over and over again without the unconscious necessarily possessing any 'reasonable' purpose. Whatever the case may be, the result of repetition compulsion may be that the conscious desire for change is transformed through the situations to a repetition of the traumatic event, sometimes with the possibility of an alternative and perhaps more creative outcome, sometimes as a confirmation of the traumatic content of the traumatic event. Repetition compulsion is one of the mechanisms that may demonstrate how the unconscious is simultaneously destructive, creative and always insistent in its form.

The iceberg that only reveals a tiny fraction of itself above the surface is a common metaphor for the relationship between the conscious and the unconscious. The metaphor contains an understanding that there is a considerable amount of material hidden underneath the surface, and that much of what lies hidden is quite old. However, it completely misses the point that the unconscious is a vital, multifaceted and complex force field that is constantly reconfigured, finding new avenues, creating new connections and exerting new forms of pressure. Perhaps a better metaphor for the unconscious is the teeming marine life with corals, tiny colourful fish, big dangerous predators, sea anemones, plankton, debris and plastic, native bacteria, the skeleton of a sailor who fell overboard in 1878, passing whales and various forms of pollution.

The super-ego

As mentioned earlier, the super-ego is a concept that belongs to Freud's second topical model. The super-ego contains morality, conscience, feelings of guilt, representations of authority, self-observation, ideals and censorship. It represents society's requirements of the individual, but is close to the id in its primitive and uncompromising functioning (Olsen, 2002). The super-ego may be mercilessly punitive and judgemental, or it may be more flexible and encourage performances via the function of the ego-ideal. The ego-ideal consists of the introjected notions about the child's and, later, the adult's desired self-image. The ego-ideal is based on love, it provides the basis for developing a healthy narcissism to allow the ego to live in harmony with its super-ego (Gammelgård, 2017).

The super-ego is formed through interactions with the parents and other significance adults and the way in which their super-ego is expressed in their parenting and their interactions with the child and with each other – as perceived by the child. The child's super-ego is not an imprint of the parents' behaviour and explicit demands, the imperatives and prohibitions of their super-egos, but is a more dynamically developed entity that is also influenced by the child's personal form (idiom), the specific circumstances and the child's developmental level and perceptual capacity.

Freud writes,

> The super-ego, which thus takes over the power, function and even the methods of the parental agency, is however not merely its successor but actually the legitimate heir of its body ... First, however, we must dwell upon a discrepancy between the two. The super-ego seems to have made

a one-sided choice and to have picked out only the parents' strictness and severity, their prohibiting and punitive function, whereas their loving care seems not to have been taken over and maintained. If the parents have really enforced their authority with severity we can easily understand the child's in turn developing a severe super-ego. But, contrary to our expectation, experience shows that the super-ego can acquire the same characteristic of relentless severity even if the upbringing had been mild and kindly and had so far as possible avoided threats and punishments.

(Freud, 1933/1964a, p. 62)

Judy Gammelgård has used the term 'the brutal super-ego' (Gammelgård, 2017; our translation) to describe the super-ego that acts as a demanding and judgmental agency. Without a strong ego to translate the super-ego's demands into realistic and independent deliberations, the super-ego may be perceived as brutal and serve as the basis of a profound sense of loneliness, an experience, for example, of never being good enough, never receiving enough love. The super-ego contains inner representations and experiences with relationships, for example containing and tender functions of self-observation and assessments, each contributing a specific voice (Bollas, 2002 p. 24). Bollas quotes Heimann's question, 'Who is speaking, to whom, about what, and why now?' as an illustration of the many voices and messages from the many internal objects that are heard, for example in psychoanalysis. The super-ego is largely unconscious, and so there is nothing to prevent it from emitting mutually contradictory impulses. A brutal super-ego without a strong ego to modify the impossible demands of the super-ego may make it difficult to live up to one's own self-expectations. A brutal super-ego may cause the person to withdraw from relationships and situations out of fear of being deemed not-good-enough. The expectation of being found wanting may also be projected to others, so that also others do not seem to be good enough. Similarly, expectations of aggression and cruelty may also be projected on others, for example in the form of paranoia or a strong inclination to perceive others as judgmental and unnecessarily devaluing.

Object relations theory

Melanie Klein is one of Freud's most important successors and an important thinker, whom both Bion and Winnicott were inspired by in many ways. Among other issues she emphasized the understanding of the child's inherent destructive impulses and not only challenged the notion of the infant as a blank slate, a *tabula rasa*, but also an understanding that the child was born innocent. She underscored that children have, experience and express highly destructive impulses from birth. The child is at the mercy of the environment and is fearful of destruction: destruction from the environment in the form of assault or neglect or in the form of their own destructive impulses (Klein,

1952). The child does not simply suckle serenely at the mother's breast; it wants to eat, penetrate, possess and destroy. The child's destructive forces are not merely the result of inflexible parenting or traumatic events. On the contrary, it is up to the environment to understand and contain the child's full emotionality, including the destructive emotions, precisely in order to teach the child to manage and deal with these emotions. To help the child let the destructive impulses be reality-tested, digested, contained. In a sense, it is neglect toward the child's developmental psychological needs to let the child grapple with this difficult task alone, which is what we do if we deny the child's natural destructive impulses and sexuality. Klein also introduced the concept of projective identification, which we discuss in a separate section. Here, we merely want to mention that projective identification and projection are both defences and forms of communication and thus a condition for developing an understanding of others.

The repressed and the receptive unconscious

There has been a fairly overwhelming tradition for regarding the material in the unconscious as consisting of traumatic experiences, repressed unacceptable sexual and destructive impulses, shame and nasty secrets. Those are undoubtedly common elements in the unconscious.

During the 1990s and 2000s, the English psychoanalyst Christopher Bollas emphasized that the unconscious contains many forms of experiences and understandings of relations and the environment that cannot be said to constitute actual traumatic events. Bollas speaks of 'the repressed unconscious' and 'the receptive unconscious.' His concept of the repressed unconscious matches Freud's and Klein's ideas. The repressed unconscious consists of repressed material that does not reach the conscious, and whose repression too is typically repressed. He underscores that for many, the super-ego develops on the basis of traumatic experiences that any child invariably has. That is completely normal, even if it is traumatic. First of all, a normal life and a normal childhood and youth unavoidably contain experiences of betrayal, loss, grief, disappointment and so forth. Even the best parents will invariably make mistakes, get things wrong, speak harder to the child than necessary, bee to yielding and so forth, and every family has major or minor traumas that influence the child and the child's perception of him/herself in the world, and which turn into significance experiences. However, that is not, argues Bollas, an adequate understanding of the unconscious:

> '... although the repressed unconscious is one important theory of unconscious thinking, it is far too narrow a perspective and does not accord with Freud's theory of dreamwork, which is a theory of unconscious creativity. Our minds are far too complex to be about any one thing, be it a repressed idea, an id derivative, the transference, or

anything. Indeed, at any moment in psychic time if we could have a look at the unconscious symphony it would be a vast network of creative combinations.

(Bollas, 2007, p. 27)

Nettleton explains Bollas's concept of the receptive unconscious: 'The unconscious mind is constituted, not only from matrices of repressed traumatic experiences, as Freud maintained, but also from psychically significant elements of the object world, that are invited into the unconscious for creative reasons' (Nettleton, 2017, p. 47). In Freud's understanding of dreams Bollas sees the beginnings of an understanding of the unconscious, and he writes about Freud, 'he forgot that part of our unconscious that creatively fulfils our desire all the time, in daydreams, conversations, creative activity, and whatnot' (Bollas, 2011, p. 229).

The way in which the child is held and met becomes part of the child's receptive unconscious. In his book about Bollas's metapsychology Nettleton (Nettleton, 2017) uses the example of one mother who wakes up her child by gently stroking the child's cheek, allowing the child to slip quietly into a new day, while the other mother immediately opens the curtains, picks up the child and, with a cheerful voice, shows the child the world that they are about to throw themselves into (ibid.) We might add, what about the child who is the first in the family to wake up, tumbles out of bed and goes into the parents' bedroom, the parents slowly rousing before they, sleep-drunk, follow their excited toddler into the kitchen, the child fully alert and ready to take on a new, exciting day. Three different kinds of interactions, each with its own dynamic, its own basic unconscious. Three normal variations on being in the world that lead to different experiences which are held in the receptive unconscious. Every child and every family has a unique way of being a family and being in relationships. Like a familial fingerprint that undoubtedly contains difficult and destructive drive impulses and repressed traumas, but also different experiences of oneself in the world, of this particular family's way of being loving toward each other, expectations of the world and of other people and families. The range of variation within the span of normal functioning is vast.

With the concept of the receptive unconscious we can explain variations on normal unconsciousness. One person could never even imagine not being part of a group, while the other cannot imagine how group belonging might be possible. One person sees authority figures as caring – and potentially stifling – while the other sees authority figures as demanding and potentially absent. Bollas highlights interactions with the objective world, and underscores that this includes both psychological objects and real objects (Bollas, 2009, pp. 79ff.). The interaction, manipulation and experience with physical objects are also a source of experiences. All perceived objects – rattles, dummies, foot stools, beds, school desks, mopeds, walking frames – lead to experiences that are part of the receptive unconscious.

Are we born with a personality? The idiom

> The idiom of a person refers to the unique nucleus of each individual, a figuration of being that is like a kernel that can, under favourable circumstances, evolve and articulate. Human idiom is the defining essence of each subject (person), and, although all of us have some acute sense of the other's idiom, this knowledge is virtually unthinkable.
>
> (Bollas, 1989, p. 212)

Bollas operates with a concept of a core self, an understanding of the idea that we embark on life with some form of unique character, a potential, and he introduces the concept of the 'idiom' to capture this phenomenon. This innate idiom has many similarities to Winnicott's concept of the true self, which we describe in the section on inner and outer self. Jemsted explains, 'A human being is more than the sum of his instincts and passions and defences, and more than the sum of external influences. There is something deep inside us that is not relational, that is fundamentally alone' (Jemsted, 2002, p. 50). The idiom may be described as the psychological correlate to our fingerprint, innate and unique to each of us (Nettleton, 2017). The idiom may be compared to a symphony, which is something other and more than the combination of instruments and notes and people. Or to an author's unique voice and tone, a tone that cannot be derived from the individual word or of the story itself, but which one recognizes whenever one sees a text by the author. The individual and the individual's unique character are much more than the sum of the component parts, something other than the sum of experiences and innate potentials. The idiom is the individual's unique character, their unique formation of their experiences, inner as well as other. Bollas writes, 'the idiom that gives form to any human character is not a latent *content* of meaning but an *aesthetic in personality* seeking not to print out unconscious meaning, but to discover objects that conjugate into meaning-laden experience' (Bollas, 1992, p. 64 f.). The idiom is thus our individual and innate readiness to have, seek and shape experiences and objects. Not an independent and coherent form, but a unique combination of forms of experiences and the formation of experiences. The child seeks and is sought by the external world; it is not just something that comes to the passive child – it is something the child actively seeks. The child develops in the meeting with the object, which is not merely a phantasy or a mirage, but a real object, which has as a quality that it does not passively change in the meeting with the child but may change in the interaction with the child.

The idiom is a concept that it is difficult to exhaust. The idiom may be part of the explanation why children in the same family can be so different, that even twins who enter the family virtually simultaneously, also have different ways of being in the world. On the one hand, it may seem deterministic, since the idiom is simply there, but on the other hand, it can also be liberating – there is something besides the context and the family that shapes the child;

from the outset, the child is unique in him/herself. If the idiom is a concept it is difficult to exhaust, the unconscious of the id, the ego and the super-ego are even more inexhaustible, but as written above, that is probably also what makes it so inspiring. We are not in control over it, it leads to repetition, garbled word salad, fun ideas, creative impulses. The super-ego in many ways is largely associated with judgmental and punitive sanctions, but the super-ego is also what Jon Kalman captures in his descriptions of the father in a fisherman's family in Iceland during the early 20th century. His super-ego compels him to learn to swim and to buy a lifeboat because he sees that is part of his children's survival:

> For the longest time, however, Oddur had been the most careless of men when it came to safety issues, but that changed gradually, due, naturally, to the sense of responsibility that kindles within you when you have children, and are suddenly the sun and moon, the earth itself beneath the feet of a little individual, their world collapses if you die; and it's nothing but the purest selfishness – a mortal sin, unforgivable – if you disregard their safety.
> (Jón Kalman Stefánsson, 2016, 'Nordfjördur, Past,' section 4, para. 2)

Anxiety

Anxiety is a basic concept in psychoanalytic theory and the defence against anxiety is a key drive in the individual's psychology. It is unpleasant and distressing to feel anxiety. The experience is accompanied by various physical sensations, such as heart palpitations, muscle tension, dry mouth and dizziness. The psychological defence mechanisms are directed at anxiety with a view to eliminating or reducing it. In psychoanalytic theory and language, anxiety is an element of normal psychological development: a common but unpleasant state that we defend against. In psychoanalytic terminology, anxiety is thus a much broader concept than the understanding of anxiety solely as a very painful state. Anxiety is a central to the understanding of neuroses, which was Freud's term for the psychopathological spectrum he was particularly interested in. In the following, we present the mindset that characterizes mainly the classic psychoanalytic understanding of anxiety and the way in which we use the concept of anxiety in the present book.

Anxiety may have an everyday character. The natural fear of taking on major tasks or showing up on a date or on the first day of a new job. Anxiety may also be about fear of more severe or potentially severe situations, such as the fear of deserted streets, angry dogs, height, diseases or surgery. Anxiety may spring from something that may have once been rationally motivated but which has now become a pattern that is transferred to something else. Fear of dogs becomes phobias, anxiety fear of getting sick becomes burdensome eating or hygiene rituals, fear of strangers becomes a fear of leaving the home. Anxiety may also have as its primary source the fear of losing others' love or of being tested and failing. That there is a strong bodily element to anxiety is evident in the way we describe anxiety: the shakes, butterflies in the stomach, a lump in the throat, wobbly knees, hairs standing on end, goose bumps, the belly doing flip-flops. And who has not had that experience?

Like so many other of Freud's concepts, the concept of anxiety changed radically over the course of his writings. In the mid 1920s, Freud replaced his first theory of anxiety with his second theory of anxiety. In his first theory of anxiety Freud assumed that the build-up of tension, that is of libido, was the cause of anxiety, and that all experiences of anxiety had the anxiety experience of birth as their origin. He distinguished between realistic fear as something related to an external threat, and neurotic fear, where the libido is released as anxiety (Freud, 1917/1963). To our knowledge, this theory of anxiety has not had any major impact since the revision that led to the second theory of anxiety. Freud's second theory of anxiety, which he introduced during the 1920s, is described, among other places, in his Lecture no. XXXII, Anxiety and Instinctual Life (Freud, 1933/1964a). The revision is brought about by the division into the id, the ego and the super-ego. Freud writes in his 32nd lecture, 'Anxiety and instinctual life,'

> With the thesis that the ego is the sole seat of anxiety – that the ego alone can produce and feel anxiety – we have established a new and stable position from which a number of things take on a new aspect. And indeed, it is difficult to see what sense there would be in speaking of an "anxiety of the id" or in attributing a capacity for apprehensiveness to the super-ego. On the other hand, we have welcomed a desirable element of correspondence in the fact that the three main species of anxiety at, realistic, neurotic and moral, can be so easily connected with the ego's three dependent relations – to the external world, to the id and to the super-ego.
>
> (ibid., p. 85)

Further, he underscores that 'it was the anxiety that made the repression' (ibid, p. 86), which is the opposite of the assumption in the first theory of anxiety. The defence is thus a defence against the experience of anxiety. Anxiety is now seen as related to a particular situation, but later it also becomes a warning of potential danger: 'the twofold origin of anxiety – one as a direct consequence of the traumatic moment and the other as a signal threatening a repetition of such a moment' (ibid., pp. 94 f.). Freud assumed that anxiety has some connection to an original situation where anxiety developed as a reaction to perceived helplessness.

Freud thus operates with three categories of anxiety or fear: realistic, neurotic and moral. Realistic fear is related to an actual threat in the external world. Fear of deserted streets may be a realistic fear; we do not know what might happen if we are suddenly *not* alone in the street. The fear of unemployment may be quite realistic, and the fear of what is going to happen if we lose our income can be similarly so. Real fear may also involve the fear of losing security, health, life, for example as a reminder that is dangerous to be sick, but also dangerous to have surgery. To a less severe degree, anxiety is the price we pay to move beyond our comfort zone as well as signal that there is something important at stake or a signal of a (potential) external threat. We feel anxiety when we take an exam or go to a job interview, as those are situations where our competence and perhaps our personality are tested and assessed. It can make good sense to be extra cautious when we move around alone in an unfamiliar part of town.

Neurotic anxiety is a displacement of the fear of impulse breakthrough from the id to the external world. The fear of the uninhibited release of drives. Neurotic fear may take on a more complicated manifestation; the fear of being overwhelmed by desire at the sight of young girls in shorts summer dresses may change into a fear of summer days or young girls or a strikingly intense investment of energy into complaints over the immodest way young women dress. The fear of the uncontrolled expression of our own aggressive impulses may lead to the opposite – an absence of the ability to set boundaries and say no. Fear of our inner impulses lead from the internal to the external, the poor, anxious ego turns one threat into another that seems more feasible and less prone to provoking a breakdown than the immediate pressure from the id.

About moral fear or anxiety, Freud writes in his 32nd Lecture,

> Many people are unable to surmount the fear of loss of love; they never become sufficiently independent of other people's love and in this respect carry on their behaviour as infants. Fear of the super-ego should normally never cease, since, in the form of moral anxiety, it is indispensable in social relations, and only in the rarest cases can the individual become independent of human society.
>
> (Freud, 1933/1964a, pp. 88 f)

Moral anxiety is thus about complying with the super-ego's instructions and prohibitions. A necessary adaptation to the external world's expectations, for example to avoid being a sore loser, rules for social interactions and showing the necessary respect. However, the judging super-ego can also be relentless in its demands. Normal anxiety about an exam, for example, may also be accompanied by the super-egos judging and possibly contradictory requirements – you must always demonstrate that you are the best, and you should never think that you're better than anyone else. Since large parts of the super-ego are unconscious, moral anxiety is both a sensible adaptation to the external world and a primitive and unprocessed inner voice, anxiety-provoking – also in everyday situations.

Anxiety is as such both a friend and an enemy. It warns us against impulse breakthroughs, behaviour that may cause us to lose beloved objects and warns us against external threats. Anxiety has two layers, anxiety in the situation and the anxiety that is unconsciously triggered by the recollection of previous situations, which may in turn lead to a general avoidance of situations that resemble them. This fear or anxiety may be handled more or less constructively. Realistic fear may lead to both situationally relevant caution and to life-restricting strategies. A key factor is how wide and flexible the defensive repertoire is that the person has access to in the situation.

Anxiety can be so overwhelming that there is no reaction. The individual is, so to speak, at the mercy of the most primitive reaction to anxiety: freeze or flight. For the individual to engage in a reality-oriented contact with the trigger of the anxiety there has to be a form of defence that makes the anxiety tolerable. Freud emphasized the use of humour as a defence. Humour lets us approach the issue that triggers our anxiety and express the virtually unspeakable. In *Jokes and their relation to the unconscious* Freud offers an amusing and convincing discussion of the capacity of humour to serve as a creative outlet for internal contradictory and insistent inner impulses and creative ways of handling conflict situations (Freud, 1905/1960).

Defence against anxiety

Defences are used to regulate and eliminate the anxiety. Some defences are so extensive that they disrupt our contact with reality, other defences work instead to partially repress the reality. A defence can potentially serve to enable the ego to maintain its connection with reality. There is a difference between a defence that cause us to lose our eyesight in order to avoid seeing the disaster, one that destroys our ability to see the disaster and one that causes us to rationalize and convince ourselves that the disaster may be disastrous, but that we can survive. The latter is obviously the more functional option. When a traumatic event occurs and sparks anxiety, the situation invariably links up with earlier anxiety-provoking situations that, for understandable as well as seemingly inexplicable paths, are associated with the situation. Throughout our childhood and youth, as a natural part of development, we are subjected to a series of natural and normal losses, all of which will spark anxiety. Birth, separation from symbiosis, the experience of being left outside the parents' relationship with each other and anxiety of specific events and experiences, such as being left behind, punished, overlooked, bitten by a dog, kicked by a horse or locked in the bathroom by a sibling. Many traumatic but also everyday situations cause anxiety, and the child initiates a defence. That is part of a normal development. If the losses are significant or severe (perhaps in connection with a poor level or a lack of containing), the anxiety may similarly grow, and the psychological defences that need to be established have to be similarly strong in order to handle the anxiety that arises. This may form the basis of a more pathological form of anxiety and of a pathological defence. That may lead to problems later in life, if the defence becomes too extensive and/or rigid, although this point should not be understood as straightforward causality or determinism.

Thus, defence mechanisms may be maladaptive or adaptive. Adaptive defences approach reality and are sufficiently effective for us to maintain contact with reality (Sørensen, 1997). Maladaptive defences, by contrast, move away from reality, for example through denial. The psychological defence is part of normal psychological development and may be understood as the psyche's basic reaction to discomfort. Defence mechanisms are also part of the ego's unconscious method for eliminating anxiety. Defence mechanisms are also part of the child's normal development, but in adults, the defence mechanisms may continue as maladaptive solutions that limit our freedom to act or exact some other, high price (Olsen, 2002).

Defence mechanisms

Probably by now, no reader is going to be surprised that the concept of defence mechanisms is far from unambiguous. Freud's daughter Anna Freud has contributed to the development of psychoanalysis in ego-psychology: she picked up where her father left off and developed the understanding of defence mechanisms in one of her key works, *The ego and the mechanisms of defense* (A. Freud, 1993). Her categorization of defence mechanisms serves as the basis of the many existing conceptualizations and classifications of the concept. In *The ego and the mechanisms of defense*, she lists ten different mechanisms: repression, regression, reaction formation, isolation, undoing, projection, introjection, turning against the self and reversal (ibid.).

Another approach to understanding defence mechanisms may be to address them from a developmental perspective. The primitive forms that the child uses in early development: splitting, projection and denial. Next, repression and reaction formation, which can be labelled the neurotic defence mechanisms, and finally the mature mechanisms: sublimation and intellectualization (Olsen, 2002).

Melanie Klein's concepts of projection and projective identification offer a third perspective on defence mechanisms, where the emphasis is on the reality orientation and the flexibility in the use of defence mechanisms. Projection and projective identification act as very early and primitive defence mechanisms, as the child distinguishes between good and bad objects (splitting), across physical objects. The concepts of projection and projective identification also help us understand each other, store both destructive and valuable objects in each other and perhaps reclaim them and acknowledge them in ourselves (see also the section on projection and projective and perceptive identification).

Social defence mechanisms

In closing, we will briefly mention that the psychoanalytic concepts of anxiety and defences have also provided inspiration for our understanding of dynamic processes in organizations. An essential source of inspiration in this work is Menzies-Lyth, who in 1960 wrote an article on anxiety and defences in nurses' work (Menzies, 1960). The basic idea is identical with the discussion above: there are situations and contexts that cause anxiety in groups and organizations, and that anxiety is managed in the group by means of social defence mechanisms. In his book *The workplace within* Hirschhorn has described three types of social defence mechanisms: basic assumptions (with reference to Bion), covert coalitions and organizational rituals (Hirschhorn, 1990). In an inspiring anthology from 2015, Armstrong and Rustin present new thinking and practice experiences about this paradigm (Armstrong & Rustin, 2015). In a previous publication we have attempted to develop and expand a thinking on the social unconscious and defence mechanisms in groups and organizations (Bonnerup & Hasselager, 2008).

Libido

We have made the concept of the libido a key concept in our understanding of love. Libido is one of Freud's many key concepts. In his early writings he defined libido as psychological energy associated with the sexual drives. In 1920–1921 he undertook certain important revisions to his conceptual thinking and from then on defined libido as vital drives. It is this second definition of libido that we embrace and apply in our understanding of love. In this section we take a closer look at the concept. We look at the development of the concept and at how the libido is invested in an object.

The libido concept is closely related to the psychoanalytic concept of drives, which is also not a simple or straightforward concept. Judy Gammelgård explains Freud's drive concept as follows:

> The drive is a continuously flowing inner source of stimulation that in psyche is translated into a representation in the form of phantasies, representations or symbols. In other words, the drive is a concept at the boundary between somatic and psychological. It is an inner force that puts the psyche to work and demands it to do something about this inner pressure by giving it psychological form. Briefly put: a drive should not be mistaken as being purely biological.
>
> Freud distinguishes 'between instincts and drives. Instincts are with us from the beginning of life, and they follow an inherent pattern. Drives, on the other hand, develop on their way to satisfaction'.
>
> (Gammelgård, 2006, p. 206; our translation)

The development of the concept

In his early writings, Freud placed great importance on distinguishing between sexual drives from self-preservation drives. The sexual drive followed the pleasure principle, while the self-preservation drive or ego drive followed the reality principle (Olsen et al., 1976). In 1920, in *Beyond the pleasure principle*, Freud rearranged his drive theory when he introduced the concept of the death drive. From this point on, he operated with two types of drives: vital drive (Eros) and death drive (Thanatos). The libido concept was now defined as an overarching concept for sexual drives and self-preservation drives (Freud, 1921/1955b, pp. 65–144). The vital drive, Eros, represents growth, sexuality, creativity and psychological tensions. Eros 'holds together everything in the world' (ibid., p. 92). The opposite of the vital drive was defined as the death drive. The death drive is an overarching concept for the drives aimed at destruction, the annihilation of life and the end to psychological tension. The death drive is regarded as a universal principle that applies to all living beings. The death drive is one of Freud's more contested concepts, a concept that undoubtedly emerged in light of Freud's experience of the brutality and after effects of the First World War. The introduction of the concept of the death drive allowed Freud to explain – and locate – hate, aggression and destructiveness.

In *Group psychology and the analysis of the ego* from 1921, shortly after his formulation of the second drive theory, Freud says,

> Libido is an expression taken from the theory of the emotions. We call by that name the energy, regarded as a quantitative magnitude (though not at present actually measurable), of those instincts which have to do with all that may be comprised under the word 'love.' The nucleus of what we mean by love naturally consists (and this is what is commonly called love, and what the poets sing of) in sexual love with sexual union as its aim. But we do not separate from this – what in any case has a share in the name 'love' – on the one hand, self-love, and on the other, love for parents and children, friendship and love for humanity in general, and also devotion to concrete objects and to abstract ideas …, though always preserving enough of their original nature to keep their identity recognizable (as in such features as the longing for proximity, and self-sacrifice). We are of opinion, then, that language has carried out an entirely justifiable piece of unification in creating the word 'love' with its numerous uses.
>
> (Freud, 1921/1955b, p. 90)

Here we see that Freud likens libido in its later meaning (vital drive) with love, and that he operates with a broad concept of love that contains far more than just sexual love. Libido is thus a vital drive, whose aim is self-preservation and reproduction, but also, more generally, a drive to preserve the human species, coming generations, and as such in stark contrast to the death drive, the opposite of the vital drive.

The investment of libido

The libido is directed at something. Cathexis (German: *Besetzung*) is a concept Freud introduced at an early stage in the development of psychoanalysis. Cathexis represents investment in an object, charging it with psychological energy. There is a quantitative aspect to the concept, as cathexis may be increased or diminished, as well as a dynamic element, as cathexis may be withdrawn or displaced to other real objects or internal object representations. When libido is invested in an object it is psychologically active; when the libido is withdrawn, the object is inactive. In case of loss the libido is withdrawn from the lost real object and invested in its object representations as well as, probably, to other real objects and other object representations. A thorough discussion of this is found in Olsen and Køppe (1981).

We have some thoughts on the use of the concept of cathexis, which is a translation of the German *Besetzung*. *Besetzung* has a natural association to obsession, a one-sided and overwhelming preoccupation with something, a person, an idea, which it *may* involve, but *Besetzung* is also a concept that includes the completely normal process of investing libido in certain internal object representations or real objects. We use the term *investment* when we write in more everyday terms about love relations to persons, tasks and organizations and *cathexis* to refer specifically to and using libido as a concept. Investment and cathexis, as we use the terms, are thus synonyms for the same process: that libido is attached to and expressed in a relationship with an internal or external object, imagined or real.

Cathexis

The psychoanalytic concept of objects is complicated and extensive and contains multiple dimensions, discussions and positions. In the first section of the present chapter, about the unconscious, we introduce and explain the concept of objects. Objects include both physical objects and persons, and they always have both a physical aspect (the real object) and a psychological aspect – the representation of the object. In his article *On narcissism: an introduction* (Freud, 1914/1957, pp. 67–102) Freud distinguishes between ego-libido and object-libido. Ego-libido is the ego's cathexis to itself, while object-libido means the ego's cathexis of object representations. Further, Freud here distinguishes between libido directed at external objects (real objects) and libido directed at internal object representations. When libido is withdrawn from, first, real objects and, next, from object representations, it may be invested in the ego. That is what occurs in narcissism. In the same article Freud also presents the economic view of libido: if too much of the libido is invested in the object, the ego may become depleted. Also, the ego is enriched if the libido is withdrawn and reinvested in the ego (ibid.).

Libido may be directed at real objects, (internal) object representations or the ego. Libido is a drive energy that can be used and withdrawn. Libido is difficult and mobile, may shift from one object to another and from internal to external and may be withdrawn. The libido finds its way from one object to another, perhaps to a more acceptable object.

Does libido refer to internal or external processes?

It is difficult to determine whether libido cathexis is exclusively an intrapsychological process, or whether libido also flows toward real objects. In other words: is it the actual colleague the libido is invested in, or is it invested in the notion or representation of this particular, preferred colleague? It appears that Freud believed real objects could also be imbued with libido (ibid.). Cathexis in relation to the real object is expressed in the relationship. The relationship becomes psychologically active, and the other experiences the cathexis as, for example, interest, attention, care. Libido is thus relational in the sense that it is directed, expressed and experienced in a relationship. At the same time, libido is also intrapsychological, as it is the internal perception and representation of the other that is the target of the cathexis. Libido is also intrapsychological in the sense that it is directed at internal objects and internal representations of self. Internal representations of self in relation to other may also be the object of libido. Judy Gammelgård summarizes Freud's considerations on the capacity to apply cathexis to internal objects as follows: 'Self-love is a condition for extending love to include all our activities, and without self-love our very existence may be in peril' (Gammelgård, 2006, p. 207; our translation). In *Organizations in depth*, Gabriel (1999) underscores that libido, according to Freud is the vital energy that the pleasure principle operates through. When we invest libido in an endeavour, what was once an idea becomes a vital striving, an urge that requires or encourages action. This illustrates that libido is not only invested in persons but also in ideas, thoughts, endeavours, organizations (ibid., pp. 16 ff).

In summary, the concept of libido is cumbersome but it also enables us to understand how we can engage with, become preoccupied with, fall in love with or become obsessed with or simply take an interest in other people, internal or external, and thus also in ourselves. A certain form of narcissism, that is cathexis directed at internal object representations is necessary for our survival and our ability to tolerate adversity. Cathexis directed at internal objects may provide support for the beleaguered ego, which has to balance between the demands of the id, the admonishments and threats of the superego and the demands of the real world. A psychologically well-functioning individual channels relevant libido (interest, attention, love) into objects (persons, things) into the external world and the relevant and appropriate amount of libido into the internal world, into the ego and object representations. Excessive degrees of cathexis directed at internal objects will lead to a loss of reality contact and a depleted contact with others. The ability to engage in ideas, persons, tasks, organizations in the real world depends on our capacity for investing libido.

Projection, projective and perceptive identification

In this section, we introduce and define the concepts projection and projective perception, which will be familiar to some readers. To this discussion we add the concept of perceptive identification, developed by Bollas (2007). Perceptive identification occurs in extension of Klein's paranoid–schizoid and depressive positions.

Projection is a basic psychoanalytic concept. Projection is both a primitive defence and an unconscious form of communication about inner states (Klein, 1952; Gabriel, 1999; Visholm, 2004a; Stapley, 2006). To examine the concepts of projection and projective identification, we turn first to Klein's understanding of the infant's inner life and to her assumption that every child contains destructive and aggressive impulses as well as loving and constructive impulses. The parents' containment of the infant helps the infant gradually develop the ability contain their own impulses. Initially, the infant experiences the world in black and white, across biological boundaries; thus, there is 'meandgoodmummy' and 'meandbadmummy,' objects are split, and ambivalent feelings are attached to different objects. This phase of the child's development is termed the paranoid–schizoid position. In the course of the child's psychological development, the position is replaced by the depressive position, where the infant learns that both mother and child contain both good and bad objects. The infant is able to perceive whole objects instead of splitting them into good and bad. The depressive aspect of the position is related to the infant's grief/depression over not only losing the ideal, always-good mother but also having to acknowledge their own destructive elements; elements which the infant needs help to be able to understand and control. Naturally, the infant does not have access to processing these experiences verbally; the verbal terms are applied in our theoretical understanding of phenomenon. However, these are not merely phases in psychological development. They are psychological positions that remain active throughout life. They possess distinctive properties as positions that an individual may fluctuate between: simplified and without ambivalence and nuances versus complex, ambivalent, complicated and sad. Each position is necessary and relevant, dependent on context and task. Projections and projective identifications are continuous inner and relational processes that enable us to understand and misunderstand each other (Klein, 1952; Hinshelwood, 1991; Bion, 1968). Projection springs from a desire to get rid of something undesirable. Something that causes anxiety. That may be the experience of possessing destructive impulses, but it may also be the experience of possessing valuable internal objects that one has to have others carry and safeguard, lest one destroy them. The projector projects the undesired material into someone else. Here, its 'fate' may vary.

The recipient of the projection may identify with the projected material, leading to projective identification: thus, the recipient identifies with the projection and makes it their own. The identification may be temporary, as the recipient detects an alien character in the experience of certain emotions or a sense of being perceived and 'framed' in a way that differs from their self-perception. The projection may also form a more permanent pattern, as the recipient of the projection continues to identify with the projected object, incorporating it into their self-perception. If the recipient projects their own anxiety-producing material into the other, who in turn identifies with it, the result is collusion. Collusion occurs when both parties carry and express parts of the other's personality, thus relieving each other of the burden but also, in the long term, depleting each other.

The recipient may also reject the projected object. Either because they fail to discover the projection, or because the projected material also provokes anxiety in the recipient, triggering a defence in the form of rejection. This compels the projector to reinternalize the projection, now perhaps confirmed as being terrible by the recipient's anxious rejection. This exacerbates the burden for the projector.

The third response to projection is to contain it. The recipient notes that they are the recipient of material that is not their own, but which the projector appeared incapable of containing. The recipient carries and processes the projected material and returns it to the projector in a form and at a time when they are able to contain it (again). To contain others' emotions, the container has to be able to 1) be in contact with the emotion, temporarily experiencing and identifying with it; 2) detect that the emotion is not their own; 3) understand the emotion and perhaps also why it is being projected; 4) carry; 5) process the projection; and, finally, 6) returning the projected material at a time and in a form that make it possible for the projector to reintroject their projections.

This third response is no small task. It is a major endeavour that requires sufficient personal insight to be able to explore the source of the emotions arising in the situation, to grasp and examine complex dynamic processes and, not least, to find it necessary, relevant and rewarding to take on the task of containment.

Containment is not unbounded. It involves drawing boundaries around the contained material – what is considered part of the task, the role, the relationship? Not in a moral sense; there may be situations where it is relevant to understand why one is called a useless moron or a monster that should never have seen the light of day. It is both appropriate and necessary for a retail clerk to draw different boundaries than a pedagogue in a special-needs residential facility; indeed, in the latter context it may be crucial to examine what the young resident is seeking to communicate.

How does it work?

Projective processes are unconscious communicative processes. They may take the form of relatively simple exchanges and distributions of emotions between two people or of highly primitive and destructive processes, where one party is attributed particularly troublesome qualities and emotions. The latter is at play, for example, in bullying or scapegoating, where the parties mutually attribute destructive or undesired qualities to each other, potentially dehumanizing each other. We see this when religious or ethnic groups that have long lived peacefully side by side are suddenly incited to perceive deep-rooted differences that seem impossible to overcome or reconcile.

Projective processes may also involve the experience of bringing out the best in one another. Egged on by others' expectations of their ability to handle the situation, someone who is not generally very brave may rise to the occasion and exceed their own expectations. Someone who is not particularly creative may encourage others to express themselves by declaring their unreserved admiration for their talents; and similarly, dynamic duos in the workplace can achieve great results by building on each other's strengths rather than insisting on perfect parity in all regards. Projective processes can also be a way of accepting and promoting understanding and managing differences – but they must be linked with reality. You do not automatically become a strong swimmer because your mother says that you are good, and you do not automatically become a good speaker, because others see you as smart and competent.

The ability to understand one's own projections and to reinternalize and process them and to detect and process projections and projective identifications are not only important for the infant but play a central role in understanding others and managing conflicts, ambivalence and uncertainty.

Perceptive identification

Bollas introduces a third position: perceptive identification, which rests on the notion that the other person has an independent existence, separate and different from oneself: 'This model presupposes the jouissance of difference (not similarity) and implicitly appreciates the separateness of the object,' as Bollas writes (2007, p. 66). In a point that is particularly pertinent to the theme of this book, he underscores that perceptive identification is a precondition of mature love. In her introduction to Bollas's meta-psychology, Nettleton explains that

> ... Bollas posits a developmental stage, following the Kleinian depressive position and Winnicott's stage of transitional object use, when the child becomes aware of the integrity of the object. Bollas terms this perceptive

> identification. Winnicotts's transitional object is significant because it stands for other experiences, but in the stage of perceptive identification it is the specificity of the object itself that is crucial.
>
> (Nettleton, 2017, p. 48)

Perceptive identification is thus both a developmental phase and a position in the Kleinian sense, where the infant detects and acknowledges that the object (the other) has an independent existence. Perceptive identification refers to the ability to perceive the other's identity as separate and distinct from oneself. The other is viewed as him/herself, not as a mirror image of one's own inner projections and phantasies, but primarily in their own right. Bollas posits that in our relations with others we vary between perceptive and projective identification (Bollas, 2007; Nettleton, 2017). Bollas further explains:

> If projective identification gets inside the other, perceptive identification stands outside to perceive the other. The term 'identification' means quite different things for each concept. In projective identification, it means identifying with the object, in perceptive identification, it means perceiving the identity of the object. Both forms of knowing need to work in tandem with one another in a creative oscillation between appreciating the integrity of the object and perceiving its identity, and then projecting parts of the self into the object, a form of imagination.
>
> (Bollas, 2007, p. 68)

The child projects their own omnipotent phantasies into the father, 'the strongest (sales)man in the world,' who lives up to – and identifies with – the infant's phantasies about his omnipotence, snapping the cap off the soft-drink bottle with a flick of the wrist. Father and child share the illusion of dad's omnipotence and strength and his ability to keep the child safe. The child also projects their own destructive impulses into the father, seeing in him not only the ability to kill the scary ghosts and the ants in the bed, but even the mother if she became too troublesome. Fortunately, the father fails to live up to this latter aspect of omnipotence, and relieved, the child can to lean on a parent who is able to distinguish between ants and mothers and express his own aggressive impulses on the soccer pitch as a lethal striker on the local old boys' team.

From the perceptive position, the child's joy springs from seeing the father as someone who has his own inner world, abilities, friends and habits that that child is not a part of, and seeing the father survive intact, because he remains himself and does not always bring his little boy along. A man and a woman may project various undesired aspects of their own inner lives into one another, perhaps attributing them to differences between the sexes: the strong man and the emotional woman (collusion); but they may also appreciate each other, precisely because of these differences: one being improvisational and impulsive, the other level-headed; one being a slow-food fan, the other an avid dancer (perception).

So, this is about splitting, integrating and spotting the differences

Each of the three positions – the paranoid–schizoid, the depressive and perceptive identification – possesses unique qualities, and all three positions can be managed in a reality-oriented and relevantly reflected manner.

There is an immediately meaningful quality in recognizing oneself in someone else, but also in seeing each other in a more nuanced perspective and appreciating the differences, such as they are. From the depressive position we may adopt a nuanced view of others and of the situations that the organization needs to be able to handle. The depressive position is a good basis for learning something new about ourselves, about others and, not least, about reality. The depressive aspect is activated in the perceived responsibility for finding a common solution, the awareness that everyone has to give up something of value, and that projected material must be reintegrated. The depressive position can also lead to endless reflections and musings on possibilities. There is always a multitude of nuances to be examined.

The quality of the paranoid-schizoid position lies in the simplification it offers, the black-and-white categorization. Sometimes it is necessary to make a decision on the spot, based on incomplete facts, and it may be easier to take on the competition in a fight for market shares if a company maintains an internal assumption that not only are we the better company, we are also, essentially, better people, who deserve to win (as long as this assumption does not lead to unethical or illegal actions or cause us to lose sight of reality). The depressive position can offer a good basis for examining a situation, while the paranoid–schizoid provides a good basis for then making a decision.

From the position of perceptive identification, we can come to appreciate that others have their own unique qualities and experiences, which is a good basis for cooperation, creativity and conflict resolution. The challenge is that it takes courage and character to acknowledge others' qualities without falling prey to envy or devaluation. It takes determination and skill to try to understand what the other understands, a certain forgiving tenderness toward the other's flaws and shortcomings and acceptance of one's own and other's ambivalent feelings. Jim Krantz points out that dealing with organizational transformation calls for the ability to make relevant shifts between the paranoid–schizoid position and the depressive position (Krantz, 2001). With reference to Bollas's concept of perceptive identification we add that it is crucial to be able to switch between splitting and integration and to be aware of the differences.

The inner and outer self

Inner and outer self

That an individual has an inner, internal side as well as an outer, external side, a physical as well as a psychological nature, seems self-evident. Winnicott has written elegantly and with great insight about this dynamic of inner versus outer in his article 'Ego distortion in terms of true and false self,' using the terms true and false self (Winnicott, 1960). The true self, as he sees it, is the child's innate potential, which forms the core of the personality: 'The True Self is the theoretical position from which come the spontaneous gesture and the personal idea ... Only the true Self can be creative and only the True Self can feel real' (ibid., p. 147). He continues,

> The True Self comes from the aliveness of the body tissues and the working of body-functions, including the heart's action and breathing. It is closely linked with the idea of the Primary Process, and is, at the beginning, essentially not reactive to external stimuli, but primary. There is but little point in formulating a True Self idea except for the purpose of trying to understand the False Self, because it does no more than collect together the details of the experience of aliveness.
>
> (ibid.)

The false self is developed as a relevant and necessary shield toward the external world to safeguard the original inner, true self: 'The False Self is represented by the whole organization of the polite and mannered social attitude, a "not wearing the heart on the sleeve"' (ibid., p. 142). The false self is a facade that the child has to develop in order to protect the self against external perceptions of the child's emotions or to enable the child to feel lovable. Winnicott saw the development of the false self as a natural part of normal development and argued that the false self might also be described as 'the social self,' as suggested by the quote above. The false self may, but will not necessarily, develop into a pathological shell that prevents the true self from being expressed. The concept of the false self thus contains both an understanding that the false self in a normal psychological sense is a necessary adaptation to the external world and the understanding that the false self remains an alien entity, a false version of one's true person. The experience of being loved or seen, primarily as one's true self, is a key part of normal psychological development.

Winnicott's concepts of the true self and the false self represent a dichotomy, a distinction between inner and outer, innate versus acquired, as much as it marks a distinction between true and false. We find this distinction between innate and acquired, between an inner mental life and a necessary and potentially healthy adaptation to the external world, meaningful, and in the chapter on loneliness we have argued that some forms of loneliness may be understood precisely as the painful experience of a wide gap between inner and outer. The terms 'true' and 'false' imply a value charge and a relative ranking of the positions that we find problematic: the idea that something (inner) is genuine, while something else (outer) is fake, and that inner is per se original, and the outer a later development aimed at achieving a necessary defence. Instead we propose the concepts *inner self* and *outer self* with the same basic definition as the one presented by Winnicott above but without the value charge and the relative ranking. Briefly put, this implies that the outer self may be just as true, genuine or 'oneself' as the inner.

The shell, the shield or the barrier a person develops contains both protective and a permeable elements. We use 'membrane' as the term to refer to this boundary between inner and outer in order to indicate that it is both protective and permeable, and that it may offer varying degrees of protection and permeability. The membrane may be highly resistant to outside input – a shield – which may be profoundly unhelpful in establishing more rewarding relations with others. But this particular barrier was developed by a particular individual in their contact with the external world. This person develops the best outer self this particular person can accomplish. That is far from 'false'; it is the best that was possible, even if the price is a wide gap between the inner and the outer self. In its representation to the external world, the outer self is not in complete control, but it is also not without influence. These conscious and unconscious processes, as they are expressed in the outer self, are part of the unique individual.

The inner self is just that: inner. The inner self that Bollas is inspired by in his description of the idiom (see the section on the unconscious) is the individual's unique self-perception, 'as I experience myself from the inside,' an experience of coherence and cohesion across time and across situations. An 'inner-self' that the individual can be in a dialogue with, can have continuous self-reflecting conversations with. The inner self will also form the basis for an experience of coherence and cohesion over the lifespan: even though I develop and change, I am still me at 25 and at 50, with a lifelong sense of coherence and cohesion, cf. the Danish Professor of Psychology Carsten René Jørgensen's definition of identity (Jørgensen, 2008).

Separate and connected

The child, cf. Winnicott, comes into being by being mirrored by the mother's loving gaze. The experience of being mirrored lets the child perceive him/herself as a separate, yet connected individual. The mirroring should be experienced as a mirroring of the child him/herself – a mirroring, neither a fusion nor a rejection. The mother similarly becomes the mother of this particular child when she sees herself mirrored in this particular child's gaze. Today we know that a lack of facial expressions in the relationship (for example due to depression, substance abuse or a lack of interest in the child) has a crucial negative impact on the child's ability to develop a self-perception and a sense of being a separate, well-defined individual (Hart & Schwartz, 2008). The mirroring needs to be adequate, meaning that the mother has to mirror the child in a way that matches the child's inner emotional experiences. A child who feels overwhelmed by nameless dread and who is met by a mother who perceives the child as being 'naughty' or who is herself overwhelmed by the child's emotions will have a very different experience than the child who is met by the mother's tenderness and patient reassurance.

Perceiving oneself as both separate and connected is a fundamental condition for well-being and development. Not only in infancy but throughout life. In order to be able to experience both the joy of connecting with another human being and the joy of being an independent individual. Being separate is a condition for meeting. Symbiosis is a precursor of the experience of being alone in someone else's presence and promotes the development of this capacity.

Separateness and connectedness as a condition for the individual's development was a key focus also for the psychoanalyst Esther Bick, who is known for her development of a method for observing infants. In her article 'The experience of the skin in early object-relations' (Bick, 1968) she describes how the infant may develop a defence Bick calls 'second skin.' She writes about this early developmental stage: 'in its most primitive form the parts of the personality are felt to have no binding force amongst themselves and must therefore be held together in a way that is experienced by them passively, by the skin functioning as a boundary' (ibid., p. 484).

The child's self-perception is associated with the experience of the skin as an interface between internal and external reality and as the setting for the child's fear of fragmentation. The skin, so to speak, keeps the child together. The skin is the place where the child perceives and experiences the distinction between inner and outer, internal and external. If the necessary containment is in place, the skin, in addition to being a concrete interface, is also symbolic in the sense that the child's painful or anxiety-filled experiences (cold or hunger, for example) are understood, managed and made tolerable. This containing function is a necessary condition for the child's development, but in some situations, it may fail or be absent. In the absence of 'psychological skin' or relevant containment the child may develop a sort of pseudo-protection, which Bick calls 'second skin':

> Disturbance in the primal skin function can lead to a development of a 'second-skin' formation through which dependence on the object is replaced by a pseudo-independence, by the inappropriate use of certain mental functions, or perhaps innate talents, for the purpose of creating a substitute for this skin container function.
>
> (ibid.)

Lucey (2015) suggests that second-skin behaviour also occurs in organizational life when there is no or insufficient containment. In that case, she argues, a similar hard shell may develop that, like other psychological defences, offers some relief from the anxiety that is present – but at a cost. This type of second-skin functioning has the following characteristics, among others:

- Relating takes place at surface level
- The second skin may make the person look strong on the outside, but they are actually fragile within
- When the second skin breaks down, there is a sudden collapse, like the rupture of a boundary
- The second skin masks real issues, which leads to distortions that, in turn, interfere with the capacity for containment(ibid., p.217)

Inner and outer self and the membrane

Lucey's examples above of 'second-skin behaviour in organizations may be understood as a result of major differences between the inner and the outer self. The concept of second-skin behaviour has also made us aware that there is a boundary between inner and other, internal and external; a boundary that is active. Inner and outer are separated and connected on the boundary. The concept of the 'skin' – the membrane (as a physical as well as perceived boundary) illustrates that this simultaneous separation and connectedness, the membrane, is an active and dynamic process. In Lucey's examples from organizations, the membrane is a highly impermeable layer that lets very little cross or filter through the boundary between inner and outer.

The membrane as a dynamic active boundary allows some things to pass through, but does not let it pass through unhindered or unmodified. The membrane is shaped by both internal and external phenomena and may thus be more or less adaptive in the way it functions – sometimes too impenetrable to external input, as illustrated by the concepts of second skin and second-skin behaviour. A membrane that is too porous, on the other hand, which lets too much of the inner self be expressed unmediated in the external world, is similarly problematic. In the latter case there is basically no protection of the inner self in the face of external pressures, and no or little censorship in relation to what it is helpful to present and express in the external world. Many of these processes are unconscious, but it is possible to express and consider them in a conscious and fairly concrete manner.

References

Armstrong, D., & Rustin, M. (2015). *Social defences against anxiety*. London, UK: Karnac.

Bick, E. (1968). The experience of skin. *International Journal of Psycho-analysis*, 49: 484–486.
Bion, W. (1962). The psycho-analytic study of thinking. *International Journal of Psycho-analysis*, 43: 306–310.
Bion, W. (1968). *Experiences in groups.* London, UK: Tavistock.
Bollas, C. (1987). *The shadow of the object. Psychoanalysis of the unthought known.* New York, NY: Columbia University Press.
Bollas, C. (1989). *Forces of destiny. Psychoanalysis and human idiom.* London, UK: Free Association.
Bollas, C. (1992). *Being a character.* London, UK/New York, NY: Routledge.
Bollas, C. (2002). *Free association.* London, UK: Icon.
Bollas, C. (2007). *The Freudian moment.* London, UK: Karnac.
Bollas, C. (2009). *The evocative object world.* London, UK/New York, NY: Routledge.
Bollas, C. (2011). *The Christopher Bollas reader.* New York, NY: Routledge.
Bonnerup, B., & Hasselager, A. (2008). *Gruppen på arbejde.* Copenhagen, Denmark: Hans Reitzels Forlag.
Budtz Pedersen, D., & Collin, F. (2015). Kampen om mennesket. Fire subjektbegreber i humanistisk forskning. In D. Budtz Pedersen, F. Stjernfelt, & S. Køppe (Eds.), *Kampen om disciplinerne.* Copenhagen, Denmark: Hans Reitzels Forlag.
Freud, A. (1993). *The ego and the mechanisms of defence.* London, UK: Karnac. (Original work published 1936.)
Freud, S. (1953a). The interpretation of dreams (first part). In J. Strachey (Ed. and Trans.), *The standard edition of the complete psychological works of Sigmund Freud (Vol. 4).* London, UK: Hogarth. (Original work published 1900.)
Freud, S. (1953b). The interpretation of dreams (second part) and on dreams. In J. Strachey (Ed. and Trans.), *The standard edition of the complete psychological works of Sigmund Freud (Vol. 5).* London, UK: Hogarth. (Original work published 1900.)
Freud, S. (1955a). An infantile neurosis and other works. In J. Strachey (Ed. and Trans.), *The standard edition of the complete psychological works of Sigmund Freud (Vol. 17).* London, UK: Hogarth. (Original work published in 1917–1919.)
Freud, S. (1955b). Beyond the pleasure principle, group psychology and other works. In J. Strachey (Ed. and Trans.), *The standard edition of the complete psychological works of Sigmund Freud (Vol. 18).* London, UK: Hogarth. (Original work published 1920–1922.)
Freud, S. (1957). On the history of the psycho-analytic movement, papers on metapsychology and other work. In J. Strachey (Ed. and Trans.), *The standard edition of the complete psychological works of Sigmund Freud (Vol. 14).* London, UK: Hogarth. (Original work published 1914–1916.)
Freud, S. (1960). Jokes and their relation to the unconscious. In J. Strachey (Ed. and Trans.), *The standard edition of the complete psychological works of Sigmund Freud (Vol. 8).* London, UK: Hogarth. (Original work published 1905.)
Freud, S. (1961). The ego and the ID and other works. In J. Strachey (Ed. and Trans.), *The standard edition of the complete psychological works of Sigmund Freud (Vol. 19).* London, UK: Hogarth. (Original work published 1923–1925.)
Freud, S. (1963). Introductory lectures on psycho-analysis (Parts I and II). In J. Strachey (Ed. and Trans.), *The standard edition of the complete psychological works of Sigmund Freud (Vol. 15).* London, UK: Hogarth. (Original work published 1915–1916.)

Freud, S. (1964a). New introductory lectures on psycho-analysis and other works. In J. Strachey (Ed. and Trans.), *The standard edition of the complete psychological works of Sigmund Freud (Vol. 22)*. London, UK: Hogarth. (Original work published 1933.)

Freud, S. (1964b). Moses and monotheism, an outline of psycho-analysis and other work. In J. Strachey (Ed. and Trans.), *The standard edition of the complete psychological works of Sigmund Freud (Vol. 23)*. London, UK: Hogarth. (Original work published 1937–1939.)

Gabriel, Y. (1999). *Organizations in depth*. London, UK: Sage.

Gammelgård, J. (2006). Gentagelsestvang og dødsdrift. In O. A. Olsen et al. (Eds.), *Fokus på Freud*. Copenhagen, Denmark: Hans Reitzels Forlag.

Gammelgård, J. (2011). Psykoanalyse. In B. Karpatschof, & B. Katzenelson (Eds.), *Klassisk og moderne psykologisk teori*. Copenhagen, Denmark: Hans Reitzels Forlag.

Gammelgård, J. (2017). *Om psykoanalyse*. Lecture at MPO, Roskilde University, 25 January.

Hart, S., & Schwartz, R. (2008). *Fra interaktion til relation*. Copenhagen, Denmark: Hans Reitzels Forlag.

Heiman, P. (1956). Dynamics of transference interpretations. *International Journal of Psycho-analysis*, 37: 303–310.

Hinshelwood, R. D. (1991). Entry 10. Depressive position and Entry 11. Paranoid-schizoid position. In R. D. Hinshelwood (1991). *A dictionary of Kleinian thought* (pp.138–166). London, UK: Free Association Books.

Hirschhorn, L. (1990). *The workplace within. Psychodynamics of organizational life*. Cambridge, MA/London, UK: The MIT Press.

Jemsted, A. (2002). Idiom, intuition and unconscious intelligence. Thoughts on some aspects of the writings of Christopher Bollas. In J. Scalia (Ed.), *The vitality of objects*. London, UK: Continuum.

Jemsted, A. (2011). Introduction. In C. Bollas (Ed.), *The Christopher Bollas reader*. New York, NY: Routledge.

Jørgensen, C. R. (2008). *Identitet*. Copenhagen, Denmark: Hans Reitzels Forlag.

Karpatschof, B., & Katzenelson, B. (2011). *Klassisk og moderne psykologisk teori*. Copenhagen, Denmark: Hans Reitzels Forlag.

Klein, M. (1952). *The writings of Melanie Klein, Volume 8: Envy and gratitude and other works*. London, UK: Hogarth.

Krantz, J. (2001). Dilemmas of organizational change: A systems psychodynamic perception. In L. Gould, L. F. Stapley, & M. Stein (Eds.), *The systems psychodynamics of organizations*. London, UK: Karnac.

Køppe, S. (2002). Strukturel synsvinkel. In O. A. Olsen (Ed.), *Psykodynamisk leksikon*. Copenhagen, Denmark: Gyldendal.

Lucey, A. (2015). Corporate cultures and inner conflicts. In D. Armstrong, & M. Rustin (Eds.), *Social defences against anxiety. Explorations in a paradigm*. London, UK: Karnac.

Menzies, I. (1960). A case study in the functioning of social systems as a defence against anxiety: A report on a study of the nursing service of a general hospital. *Human Relations*, 13(2), 95–121.

Nettleton, S. (2017). *The metapsychology of Christopher Bollas. An Introduction*. London, UK/New York, NY: Routledge.

Olsen, O. A., *et al.* (1976). Redaktionel indledning. In S. Freud (Ed.), *Metapsykologi II*. Copenhagen, Denmark: Hans Reitzels Forlag.
Olsen, O. A., & Køppe, S. (1981). *Freuds psykoanalyse*. Copenhagen, Denmark: Gyldendal.
Olsen, O. A. (Ed.) (2002). *Psykodynamisk leksikon*. Copenhagen, Denmark: Gyldendal.
Olsen, O. A., & Vedfelt, O. (2002). Det ubevidste. In O. A. Olsen (Ed.), *Psykodynamisk leksikon*. Copenhagen, Denmark: Gyldendal.
Olsen, O. A., Thomsen, C. B., & Petersen, B. (2006). *Fokus på Freud*. Copenhagen, Denmark: Hans Reitzels Forlag.
Rösing, L. M. (2007). *Autoritetens genkomst*. Copenhagen, Denmark: Tiderne skifter.
Scalia, J. (2002). (Ed.). *The vitality of objects*. London, UK: Continuum.
Stapley, L. (2006). *Individuals, groups and organizations beneath the surface: An introduction*. London, UK: Karnac.
Stefansson, J. K. (2016). *Fish have no feet*. London, UK: MacLehose Press. (Kindle DX version). Retrieved from www.amazon.com.
Sørensen (1997). Psykisk forsvarsorganisation. In S. Lunn (Ed.), *Om psykoanalytisk kultur*. Copenhagen, Denmark: Dansk Psykologisk Forlag.
Thielst, P. (2006). Det man ikke er sig bevidst. In O. A. Olsen (Ed.), *Fokus på Freud*. Copenhagen, Denmark: Hans Reitzels Forlag.
Visholm, S. (2004a). Organisationspsykologi og psykodynamisk systemteori. In T. Heinskou, & S. Visholm (Eds.), *Psykodynamisk organisationspsykologi. På arbejde under overfladen*. Copenhagen, Denmark: Hans Reitzels Forlag.
Visholm, S. (2004b). Modstand mod forandring – psykodynamiske perspektiver. In T. Heinskou, & S. Visholm (Eds.), *Psykodynamisk organisationspsykologi. På arbejde under overfladen*. Copenhagen, Denmark: Hans Reitzels Forlag.
Winnicott, D. (1960). Ego distortion in terms of true and false self. In D. Winnicott (1964). *The maturational processes and the facilitating environment (Chapter 12)*. London, UK: Karnac.
Zeuthen, K. & Køppe, S. (2014). Nyere psykoanalytiske teorier. In S. Køppe, & J. Dammeyer (Eds.), *Personlighedspsykologi. En grundbog om personlighed og subjektivitet*. Copenhagen, Denmark: Hans Reitzels Forlag.
Zeuthen, K. *et al.* (2008). Tilknytning og udviklingens drivkraft. *Psyke & Logos, 29(2)*, 431–450.

Index

afterwardsness 118
alone 22, 60, 74, 77–80, 94, 141
ambivalence 16–17, 26, 33–4, 58, 134, 136
anxiety 19, 85–9, 108, 111, 116, 125–30, 135

being alone 22, 60, 68, 77–80, 83–4, 94–100, 102–03
Besetzung 132
betrayal 29, 45, 55, 122
Bick, E. 81, 141
Bion, W.R. 43, 78–80, 111, 117, 119, 121, 130, 134
Bollas, C. 20–21, 29, 51, 117, 121–24, 134–40
brutal super-ego 89, 93, 121

cathexis 15, 17–18, 132–34
capacity to be alone 77–80, 90, 94, 103, 112
changeling 85, 91–4
collegial relations 22, 71, 75
collusion 26, 29–33, 39, 135, 137
connectedness 141–42
containing 45, 81, 111, 117, 121, 128, 135, 141
containment 134–35, 141–42
creative pair 34, 37, 39–42, 45–6
creativity 41–2, 45–6, 50, 54, 122, 131, 138
critical thinking 71

defence mechanisms 31, 116, 118, 125, 129–30
defences 36, 85, 122, 124, 128–30
delegate 31, 104–07
delegation 31–2, 104–08, 111
depressive position 21, 134, 136, 138
differentiation 17–19
drives 13, 17, 117–18, 127, 130–31

ego 14, 23, 115–18, 125–29, 131–34
ego-ideal 22–3, 54, 89, 120
ego-libido 132
emotional style 70
emotions 12, 17, 20–3, 29–31, 41, 45, 60, 69–71, 78, 81–2, 103–04, 111, 136
exclusive pair 34

failure 22, 51–2, 55, 72
false self 81, 139
fear 39, 44, 79, 81, 89–91, 117, 119, 125–28, 141
fear of disclosure 72, 109
fear of exposure 72, 85, 87–91, 97
feelings 34, 45, 68, 84–6, 120, 134, 138
formal and informal pairs 25–6, 33–4
French, R. 24, 26–28
Freud, S. 13–15, 17–19, 22, 59, 85, 89, 115–33
Freud, A. 129
friendship 6, 10, 18, 26–9, 33, 39–41, 52, 67, 131
friendship pair 24–8, 34, 37–9, 45–6
Fromm, E. 15, 17
fusion 17–19, 140

group dynamics 34, 44, 104
guilt 68, 120

holding 41
'homo sentimentalis' 69

id 89, 115–18, 120, 122, 125–27, 133
idealization 35, 45, 54, 98, 102, 104, 108–09
idiom 120, 124–25, 140
individualization 73–4
inner and outer self 85, 124, 139, 142
inner conflicts 30–1, 51

inner self 81–5, 90, 98, 140, 142
intimacy 21, 27, 30, 38, 55
investment 18, 20, 23, 27, 38, 63, 127, 132

Kernberg, O. 13, 15–17, 22, 37
Klein, M. 19–21, 30, 108, 116, 121–22, 129, 134, 136–37

leader 50, 56, 59, 61–3, 94–5, 98–100
libidinal centre 58, 62–4
libido 13–17, 22–3, 26, 33–9, 59–61, 63–4, 108, 116–17, 126, 130–34
loneliness 1, 67
lonely 60, 67–8, 73, 77–80, 83–5, 90–5, 97–8, 100–04, 111
love, the concept of 10–12, 17, 24, 64
love of the group 58–61, 64
love of the organization 58
love of the task 46, 48, 50, 52, 57, 64

marriage of convenience 34–8, 45
mature 16, 18, 21, 77, 83, 101–02, 129, 136
membrane 140, 142
Menzies-Lyth, I. 130
mother-child couple 17–20, 24, 41, 49, 77–8, 116, 122–23, 140–41
moral anxiety 127
mortality 68

Nachträglichkeit 118
nameless dread 78–9, 90, 119, 141
neurotic anxiety 127

object 14, 17–22, 29–31, 33, 35, 37, 58–9, 79, 81, 90, 103, 108–9, 116, 121, 123–4, 128–37, 141
object relations 19–20, 116, 121–22
other, the 14–23, 25, 27, 29, 33, 124, 126, 133, 135–38
outer self 81–6, 90, 98–9, 124, 139–40, 142

pair as group dynamic 42
pairs in working life 33
paranoid-schizoid position 134, 138
passion 46–50, 52–5, 57–8, 64, 81, 92–3, 124

perceptive identification 19–21, 29, 37–8, 64, 94, 129, 134, 136–8
personality 30, 37, 46, 69–71, 77, 79–80, 83–4, 91, 124, 127, 135, 139, 141
phantasies 21, 24, 81, 118–19, 137
play 40–3, 63
pleasure principle 131, 133
positive thinking 71
potential space 41–2
projection 15, 19–21, 26, 29, 37, 60, 64, 79, 94, 98–100, 109, 122, 129, 134–37
projective identification 19–21, 29, 37–8, 64, 122, 129, 134–37
psychological apparatus 115
psychological skin 141–42

realistic anxiety 125–28
receptive unconscious, the 122–23
repetition compulsion 119–20
repressed unconscious, the 81, 115, 118, 122–3
responsibility 17, 70, 74, 80, 109
role 25–28, 31–34, 67, 69, 74, 76–7, 84, 94–5, 98–104, 112, 135
romantic couple 24, 26, 42

scapegoat 91, 94, 104, 108–9, 136
second skin 81, 141–42
self-appreciation 22
self-love 22, 131, 133
separateness 15, 21, 136, 141
shame 68–9, 77, 85, 87–9, 122
social defence mechanisms 130
solitude 68, 75, 77–8, 95
super-ego 22–3, 50–1, 54, 59, 72, 86, 89–90, 93, 115–17, 120–22, 125–27

tenderness 14–17, 22, 26, 37–8, 138, 141
transgenerational 100
transitional object 136–37
trauma 58, 100, 118–20, 122–23, 126, 128
true self 124, 139

unconscious, the 14, 29, 31–2, 34, 50, 79, 81–2, 104–05, 109–10, 115–25

Winnicott, D. 19, 20, 41, 48, 55, 77–9, 81–2, 121, 124, 136–7, 139–40